BUILDING RESILIENCY
in Youth

A Trauma-Informed Guide
for Working with Youth in Schools

Also from the Boys Town Press

Building Resiliency in Teens: A Trauma-Informed Workbook for Teens
Building Resiliency in Children: A Trauma-Informed Activity Guide for Children
Teaching Social Skills to Youth, 3rd Ed.
Teaching Social Skills to Youth with Mental Health Disorders
Well-Managed Schools, 2nd Ed.
Tools for Teaching Social Skills in School
More Tools for Teaching Social Skills in School
Everyone's Talking
Take Two: Skill-Building Skits You Have Time to Do!
13 & Counting: Be the Difference
13 & Counting: Does a Hamburger Really Have to Be Round?
13 & Counting: Rescue Me
GRIT & Bear It!
GRIT & Bear It! Activity Guide
Zest: Live It
Zest: Live It Activity Guide
Effective Study Strategies for Every Classroom
Positive Alternatives to Suspension
School Administrator's Resource Guide
Working with Aggressive Youth
Adolescence and Other Temporary Mental Disorders (DVD)
No Room for Bullies
Safe and Healthy Secondary Schools
Common Sense Parenting®

For Adolescents
He's Not Just Teasing!
Am I Weird?
I Lost My BFF
Middle School Misfits: The Stained Glass Tree
Friend Me!
Dating!
Boundaries: A Guide for Teens
A Good Friend
Basic Social Skills for Youth

For a free Boys Town Press catalog, call 1-800-282-6657
Visit our website at BoysTownPress.org

Boys Town National Hotline®
1-800-448-3000
A crisis, resource, and referral number for kids and parents

BUILDING RESILIENCY
in *Youth*

A Trauma-Informed Guide for Working with Youth in Schools

Kat McGrady, ED.D., LCPC, NCC

Boys Town, Nebraska

**Building Resiliency in Youth: A Trauma-Informed Guide
for Working with Youth in Schools**

Published by Boys Town Press
Boys Town, NE 68010

ISBN: 978-1-944882-78-5

Boys Town Press is the publishing division of Boys Town, a national organization serving children and families.

Publisher's Cataloging in Publication

Names: McGrady, Kat, author.

Title: Building resiliency in youth : a trauma-informed guide for working with youth in schools / Kat McGrady.

Description: Boys Town, NE : Boys Town Press, [2021] | Accompanied by two activity workbooks: "Building Resiliency in Children: A Trauma-Informed Activity Guide for Children" (includes 33 adult-led activities for children ages 5-12) and "Building Resiliency in Teens: A Trauma-Informed Workbook for Teens" (includes 27 self-guided assessments and activities for middle and high-school aged children). | Includes bibliographical references and index.

Identifiers: ISBN: 978-1-944882-78-5 (guide) | 978-1-94488279-2 (children's workbook) | 978-1-94488280-8 (teen workbook)

Subjects: LCSH: Children--Counseling of. | Social work with children. | Teenagers--Counseling of. | Social work with teenagers. | Psychic trauma--Treatment. | Traumatic incident reduction. | Post-traumatic stress disorder in adolescence--Treatment. | Post-traumatic stress disorder in children--Treatment. | Resilience (Personality trait) in adolescence--Study and teaching. | Resilience (Personality trait) in children--Study and teaching. | School psychology. | BISAC: EDUCATION / Counseling / Crisis Management, | EDUCATION / Educational Psychology. | EDUCATION / Professional Development. | PSYCHOLOGY / Mental Health.

Classification: LCC: RJ506.P55 M34 2021 | DDC: 618.92/8521--dc23

10 9 8 7 6 5 4 3 2 1

How to Use This Guide

This guide is included in a set of resources designed to inform adults working with children and/or teens who have encountered trauma or other hardships. The entire resource kit includes: (a) this guide, which serves as a support for professionals, (b) an *Activity Guide for Children*, including a children's read-aloud with accompanying activities and prompts for conversation, and (c) a *Workbook for Teens*, which can be used either in groups or independently. For more details on the additional components of this kit, see the *Appendix* section.

This guide has been broken down into two general sections, each section containing multiple modules:

- One universal section, meant to benefit and inform all roles, and
- One leadership-focused section, tailored towards those who wish to train others.

The table below outlines the modules within each section, intended audience, and page number for your reference. Additionally, in order to further define the intended purpose of these modules, a snapshot of each is located in *Breakdown of this Guide*.

Table of Contents

Table of Contents (continued)

PART 3: APPENDIX

– AUDIENCE –

Practitioners who opted to use supplemental pieces of kit (Workbook for Teens, Activities for Children, or children's read-aloud)

PART 1
Universal Resource

Breakdown of This Guide

As stated in previous pages, this guide is broken down into modules. For quick reference and ease of use, a snapshot of each module is listed below. Following each subtitle/module listed, you will find a brief description of the material contained within. These snapshots may be used to expeditiously locate information and resources that meet specific needs or foci.

WHAT IS TRAUMA?

Provides a research-based definition, elements, and overarching understanding of trauma.

TYPES OF TRAUMA

Identifies the various types of trauma as defined by current research.

THE IMPACT OF TRAUMA

Identifies some of the most prevalent social, emotional, behavioral, mental, and physical influences of trauma on youth, as well as "look fors" to assist in identifying those children and teens who may have been, or continue to be, impacted by traumatic events.

KEY ELEMENTS OF BECOMING A TRAUMA-INFORMED PROFESSIONAL

Examines key elements necessary for becoming a trauma-informed professional within the culture of a trauma-informed work environment. Ideas, concepts, and tips for strengthening your ability to work with children and teens who have been impacted by trauma will be discussed.

THE BRILLIANTLY RESILIENT BRAIN: PLASTICITY

Breaks down how the brain works, neuroplasticity, and implications when working with children/teens who have been impacted by trauma.

SNAP SKILLS: RESILIENCE-STRENGTHENING

Outlines tips and ideas for strengthening resilience in children and teens.

SNAP SKILLS: TECHNIQUES AND STRATEGIES

Includes a comprehensive snapshot of coping tools and strategies to use with youth, as needed.

TIPS FOR PRESENTING TO STAFF & SUPPORTS

Provides research-based ideas for leaders who plan on providing quality and purposeful professional development (PD) or training on trauma and resilience to staff/community/ other supporters.

POSSIBLE TOPICS/OUTLINE OF TALKING POINTS FOR PD SESSIONS

Describes snapshot ideas for presenting trauma-informed PD to staff/community/other supporters.

COMPASSION FATIGUE AND HOW TO AVOID IT

Outlines information on compassion fatigue including: "look fors," ways to recognize when compassion fatigue is impacting you, and ways to stop, or ease, this phenomenon.

CHILDREN'S ACTIVITIES AND TEEN WORKBOOK: PURPOSE AND USE

For those who choose to use the accompanying Activity Guide for Children and Workbook for Teens, a brief explanation of each is provided, including why and how to use them, as well as a few sample activities from each.

REFERENCES FOR FOLLOW UP AND/OR PROFESSIONAL DEVELOPMENT TRAINING

Lists resources, references, and guides to extend understanding of trauma, trauma-informed practice, and implementation of successful professional development training.

Benefits of
This Guide

Thank you for taking the time to read and reflect on the information presented in this guide. By familiarizing yourself with the research, subject matters, and versatile methodologies described here, you are taking essential strides towards enhancing your ability to provide the quality support and care necessary for positive and productive growth in children and teens facing adversity.

This guide will strengthen your foundational understanding of:

- trauma,
- grit and resilience,
- how to recognize and best support individuals who have been impacted by trauma,
- how to reach impacted youth through a variety of approaches,
- how to encourage and cultivate resilience,
- how to practice intentional reflection,
- compassion fatigue and methods to alleviate the effects, and
- how to provide exceptional trauma-informed professional development and training.

Acquainting yourself with the information provided in this guide will also limit the possibility of inadvertent re-traumatization or added emotional duress that could be induced by ill-informed courses of action. We do not always know what goes on behind the scenes, or once children leave our sight. We do not always know what they have experienced, or the mark that their experiences may have left on them. The more enlightened you are with: (a) trauma, (b) the overall impact of trauma on a developing child/teen, and (c) best practices for fostering resilience/overcoming adversities, the more effective you will be in promoting long-term overall well-being.

There are several first-rate resiliency and trauma-focused resources currently available. Many of these resources focus on defining and identifying key aspects of trauma and resilience, yet, few expand on this by providing specifics as to how to support youth in overcoming trauma and in strengthening resilience. Moreover, caretakers and professionals alike often express that they have obtained the "what/who/why" when it comes to trauma and resilience, but they are left to their own devices when it comes to the details as to "now what." Hence, this guide has been structured to primarily focus on:

- concrete and user-friendly strategies for supporting children/teens in building resilience and the skills to counteract trauma,

- how to provide quality trauma-informed and resiliency-centered professional development, as well as meaningful follow up to ensure enduring effectiveness,

- how to recognize and combat compassion fatigue, and

- highlighting of other available literature to further expand on your proficiency and skills.

Keywords/ Definitions

Select words and terms used in this guide may be somewhat subjective or have variants based on context. In an effort to avoid possible misinterpretation, a list of fundamental, yet broadly translated expressions are defined below. Please note that these definitions are meant to provide clarity within this guide and therefore may not fully align with those found in other books, articles, or materials.

CHILD:

For the purpose of this guide, the term child will be defined as any human being between the ages of 4-12, or the developmental age that falls between birth/toddler and teenager.

COMPASSION FATIGUE:

The American Institute of Stress (AIS) defines compassion fatigue as "the emotional residue or strain of exposure to working with those suffering from the consequences of traumatic events. It differs from burn-out but can co-exist."

(Retrieved from https://www.stress.org/military/for-practitionersleaders/compassion-fatigue)

PROFESSIONAL LEARNERS:

For the purpose of this guide, professional learners will be defined as those learning and growing in the area of trauma-informed care.

RESILIENCY:

For the purpose of this guide, resiliency will be defined as the learned skill or ability to overcome challenges or life-altering events and experiences, as well as the ability to grow and to strengthen one's self in the aftermath of such an event or experience.

TEEN:

For the purpose of this guide, the term teenager will be defined as an adolescent or human being between the ages of 13-19.

TOXIC STRESS:

The Center on the Developing Child defines toxic stress as "excessive or prolonged activation of stress response systems in the body and brain." This form of stress could negatively impact one's behavior, actions, and overall health throughout their lives.

(Retrieved from https://developingchild.harvard.edu/science/key-concepts/toxic-stress/)

TRAUMA:

For the purpose of this guide, trauma will be defined as a singular or a multi-occurring event that negatively impacts one's physical, mental, emotional, social, and/or overall well-being.

TRAUMA-INFORMED PRACTICE/CARE (TIC):

According to the Substance Abuse and Mental Health Services Association (SAMHSA), the definition of trauma-informed care (TIC) is the "adoption of principles and practices that promote a culture of safety, empowerment, and healing."

(Retrieved from https://www.integration.samhsa.gov/clinical-practice/trauma)

TRIGGER:

According to the University of Alberta's Sexual Assault Centre, a trigger is defined as "something that sets off a memory tape or flashback transporting the person back to the event of her/his original trauma." This trigger may be activated by one or more of the person's senses.

(Retrieved from https://psychcentral.com/lib/what-is-a-trigger/)

What Is Trauma?

Take a minute to consider a significant and unsettling experience in your life. This could be an event that was or is ongoing, or an event that occurred only once. It could be the moment that you learned of the sudden death of a loved one or the moment that you learned of a loved one being diagnosed with a terminal illness. Perhaps you experienced the unfolding of the events on September 11th or Sandy Hook. Maybe you have been the victim of domestic violence or were involved in an accident.

Where were you when you first learned of or experienced this event? What were you doing? What did you smell and hear in the background as you processed what was happening? Whom did you call for comfort?

You may vividly remember that day or event. You may not remember the event as more than a fuzzy dream but every sight, scent, smell, and feel surrounding it may be as clear as day. These memories, the pages written into our life stories that run outside the realm of our "norm," the ones that go against our understanding of the world and our place in it, the ones that rock us, those memories impact our implicit memory on a considerable

level. It is these memories that can be recalled or triggered through seemingly unconnected sensory inputs at any given time (Gertel Kraybill, 2019). When recalled or triggered, it is these memories that have a profound and undesirable impact on our thoughts, behaviors, actions, and overall well-being.

We typically see horrendous and unspeakable events as traumatic. When we hear the word "trauma," we may immediately start picturing events so harrowing that they lead us to avoid the evening news. These events are debilitating, they are unexplainable, and they often leave us questioning our understanding and perception of the world. Natural disasters, terrorism, mass shootings, violence, abuse, rape, refugee experiences… these are the experiences that are conjured up when we hear the word "trauma."

However, trauma can transpire from events that may seem relatively less significant. A family member abusing drugs or alcohol, divorce, living in impoverished or unsafe neighborhoods, social media/ cyber bullying, even the disintegration of a friendship or slipping and falling in front of a crowd of peers could be considered traumatic events in one's life.

In this sense, trauma is in the eye of the beholder. Depending on the lens with which the event is being viewed, trauma can come from a variety of frames. The impact of trauma, the way that it is viewed or the mindset that one takes on in terms of or as a result of trauma, and the way in which a traumatic event is handled or coped with, may vary from person to person.

The lens of a child and that of a teen is still developing. This lens has not had the opportunity to strengthen through life experience and resiliency-strengthening exposure to events and possible coping strategies. Therefore, a youth's understanding of the world and how to navigate through it, along with their developmentally emerging cognitive and emotional capabilities, leads to an elevated need for guidance when potentially traumatizing events occur.

For the purpose of this guide, trauma will be defined as a singular or a multi-occurring event that negatively impacts one's physical, mental, emotional, social, and/or overall well-being. It is the hope that we can capture all forms of trauma, as well as the skills and techniques necessary to counter it, by using this definition and the implications that follow.

This section explored the general definition of trauma. In the next section, we will explore the types of trauma as identified by current research and literature.

SNAPSHOT POINTS TO REMEMBER

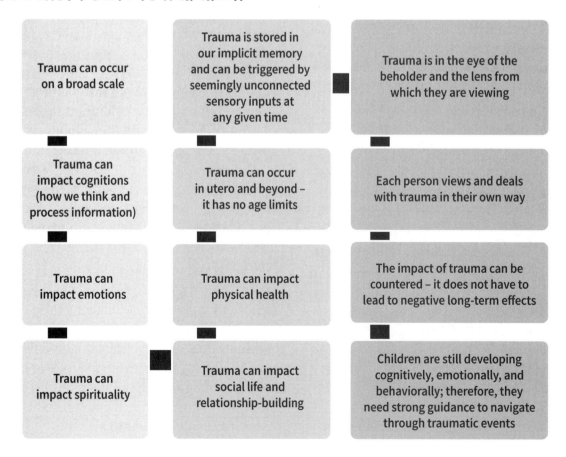

Types of Trauma

We have just explored a comprehensive definition of the term trauma. Now, we will focus on various types of trauma. We will explore the depth and breadth of, as well as possible origins of, childhood trauma.

As indicated in the previous section, trauma can occur on a broad scale. It is in the eye of the beholder and the lens from which they are viewing. While this is important to remember when supporting children/teens, the three main types of trauma that are typically recognized include:

- *Acute:* Generally defined as one event that is short-lasting.
- *Chronic:* Generally defined as multiple and prolonged events that take place over a long period of time and may be progressive.
- *Complex:* Generally defined as multiple and prolonged events that:
  - start at a young age,
  - take place over a long period of time,
  - impact one or more areas of development, and
  - that are caused by trusted adults who were responsible for the care and safety of the child.

Further, children or teens may experience trauma:

- directly, in which they experience or observe a traumatic event first-hand (e.g., neglect, abuse, bullying), or
- indirectly, in which they are impacted by an event that is not directly experienced or witnessed by them (e.g., terror attacks seen on TV, pandemics, learning that a friend's parent whom they've never met is sick).

In addition to indirect trauma, epigenetics may factor into inherited impacts of trauma. According to the Center on the Developing Child (2015), epigenomes, or chemical signatures that are encoded into our brains based on genetics and environmental factors, can impact long-term mental and physical health. Recent epigenetic studies have found that these signatures can be passed down to future generations. In other words, a parent who may have experienced complex trauma which resulted in epigenetic changes could pass these changes on to their children (Combs-Orme, 2013). This could then lead to incongruous responses to stress, heightened arousal, or difficulty in cognitive, social, emotional, or behavioral areas in these children (Cowan, Callaghan, Kan, & Richardson, 2016).

ACEs

You may have heard the acronym "ACEs" in relation to childhood trauma. The term ACEs, or Adverse Childhood Experiences, stems from a major study conducted by Dr. Vincent Felitti and Dr. Robert Anda in alliance with Kaiser Permanente's Health Clinic and with

SNAPSHOT POINTS TO REMEMBER

Types of Trauma

Acute: One event and/or short-term

Chronic: Multiple events, over time, progressive

Complex: Negatively impacts one or more areas of development, multiple events, over time, starts at a young age, caused by a caretaker

Direct: Firsthand experience or observation of an event

Indirect: Not directly experienced or observed but still feel the radiating impact of an event

the Centers for Disease Control and Prevention. This study was an eye-opening revelation when completed in 1997, as it identified three major adverse childhood experiences and their long-term impact. We will examine this study in the next section, however, it is important to note that the childhood traumatic experiences identified in this study were: abuse, neglect, and household dysfunction.

While there are numerous other experiences that could cause trauma in a child or teen, these three experiences identified in the ACEs study are important to remember, as they are strong indicators of the need for additional support.

Trauma comes in many shapes and forms and can derive from a number of experiences, both personal and secondhand. In the next section, we will explore the physical, mental, behavioral, and emotional impact of trauma.

SNAPSHOT POINTS TO REMEMBER

Major Adverse Childhood Trauma: Experiences Identified in ACEs Study

Abuse: Physical, emotional, and/or sexual

Neglect: Physical or emotional

Household Dysfunction: Mental illness in household, violence, divorce, addiction or substance abuse, etc.

The Impact
of Trauma

The previous module highlighted the various types of trauma that children and adolescents may experience. In this section, we will dig deeper into the impact of trauma. We will examine the effects of trauma on physical, behavioral, and mental health. In effect, we will explore the scope of impact on cognition, brain structure and function, social-emotional welfare, and physiological health.

The now infamous ACEs study was briefly highlighted in the previous section. This large-scale study, which spanned over the course of two years (1995-1997), sought to better understand the origins of risk factors that create negative impacts on mental health, physical health, and overall well-being. Doctors Vincent Felitti and Robert Anda, the chief researchers in the ACEs study, found that there was a strong correlation between childhood traumatic experiences (defined as abuse, neglect, or household dysfunction in this particular study) and negative long-term overall health concerns (defined as behavioral concerns, as well as physical and mental health concerns). With the support of both Kaiser Permanente's Health Clinic and the Centers for Disease Control and Prevention, Felitti and Anda discovered that adults who had encountered one or more of the adverse childhood experiences (as defined by the study) were more likely than their counterparts who had not endured an adverse childhood experience to suffer from:

- Mental health concerns such as:
  ○ Depression
  ○ Attempted suicide
  ○ Social/relationship challenges
- Physical health concerns such as:
  ○ Heart disease
  ○ COPD
  ○ Diabetes
  ○ Obesity
  ○ Cancer
  ○ Stroke
  ○ STDs
  ○ Decreased lifespan/early death
- Risky behaviors that increase physical and mental health concerns such as:
  ○ Drug use
  ○ Alcoholism
  ○ Smoking
  ○ Troubles at work/absences

(ACEs Too High, 2017; Felitti et al., 1998)

The ACEs study led to a surge in research regarding childhood trauma. As a result, there has been an expansion of knowledge on just how deeply childhood trauma can impact one's abilities and wellness, even through adulthood. We will now discuss some of these more recent studies and findings related to the impact of trauma on children and teens.

The esteemed Child Welfare Information Gateway, a service of the U.S. Department of Health and Human Services, has written extensively on the impact of childhood trauma based on comprehensive research and analysis of internal and external studies. Among their findings are the chemical and structural changes that occur in the brain when a child is exposed to trauma. These changes impact the ability to emotionally, socially, and behaviorally self-regulate. Moreover, these changes may impact cognitive ability in areas such as processing, assessing verbal cues, and communicating.

When exposed to chronic or complex trauma, the brain may become trapped in a constant state of arousal or disequilibrium. This can lead to a number of physical, mental, emotional, and cognitive complications. Badenoch (2008) explains that this constant arousal results in increased cortisol levels. This overabundance of cortisol can then kill cells in the hippocampus which houses long-term memory as well as other imperative functions. Moreover, The National Center for Child Traumatic Stress explains that this ever-present release of stress hormones leads to a chronic state of "fight or flight" mode and inability to logically process and respond to situations. Additionally, this chronic state typically results in either toxic stress and further brain damage, or to a complete shutdown of the system itself, leading to issues such as dissociation, emotional numbness, and inappropriate emotional reactions. All of which tend to lead children down a path of maladaptive behaviors (NCCTS, 2008).

Below are specific snapshot points to remember in terms of the impact of trauma on children and teens. Further information can be found in the resources listed in the References section.

SNAPSHOT POINTS TO REMEMBER

IMPACT ON THE COGNITIONS AND THE BRAIN

- Inability to retain and/or process new information
- Inability to access new learnings due to heightened state of arousal
- Impaired cognitive abilities and difficulties in school
- Decreased IQ
- Developmental delays
- Diminished executive functioning skills such as ability to focus, organize, maintain attention and concentration, impulsivity, and processing information
- Maladaptive coping mechanisms (smoking, drugs, drinking, risky sexual behaviors, etc.) can lead to even more negative impacts on cognition

POSSIBLE IMPACT ON BRAIN STRUCTURE AND FUNCTION

- Reduced volume of corpus callosum, cerebellum, and/or hippocampus
- Smaller prefrontal cortex

- Excessive reactivity of the amygdala
- Possible inability of hippocampus to bring cortisol levels back to baseline
- Abnormal cortisol and adrenaline levels
- Decreased electrical activity in the brain and brain metabolism
- Poorer interhemispheric connection or communication between key areas of the brain
- Chronic activation of neural pathways that lead to a fear response may lead to hyperarousal and persistent state of fear
- Maladaptive coping mechanisms (smoking, drugs, drinking, risky sexual behaviors, etc.) can lead to even more changes in brain structure and function

IMPACT ON BEHAVIORS

- Harder time managing emotions
- Difficulty with effective problem solving
- Increased rate of drop-out, suspensions, expulsion, or absenteeism
- Anger, frustration, sadness, irritability, moodiness
- Hyper- or hypo-arousal
- Avoidance
- Lower sense of morality and fairness
- Maladaptive coping mechanisms (smoking, drugs, drinking, risky sexual behaviors, etc.) can lead to even more negative behaviors and actions

SOCIAL-EMOTIONAL IMPACT

- Social withdrawal or isolation
- Attachment disorders
- Inability to read and properly respond to social cues/lack of social attunement
- Difficulty with redirection or criticism
- Difficulty with authority or boundaries

- Difficulty regulating emotions (identifying emotions, communicating needs in a healthy manner)
- Difficulty experiencing empathy for others
- Lack of self-esteem, confidence, and self-awareness
- Difficulty gaining sense of self
- Extreme feelings of guilt or shame
- Maladaptive coping mechanisms (smoking, drugs, drinking, risky sexual behaviors, etc.) can lead to even more negative social-emotional behaviors and mindsets

PHYSIOLOGICAL IMPACT

- Impact on sleep, eating, and general daily necessities which can lead to short- and long-term health issues
- Impaired sensorimotor development
- Increased medical and somatic symptoms
- Constant state of high-alert, fear, worry, or anxiety, which can lead to short- and long-term health issues
- Maladaptive coping mechanisms (smoking, drugs, drinking, risky sexual behaviors, etc.) can lead to even more negative impacts on the body and function

ACES CONNECTION

- When compared to counterparts who did not ensure adverse childhood experiences, those who had are more likely to:
  - Experiment with and/or to become addicted to drugs, smoking, or alcohol
  - Miss work and be less productive
  - Become obese
  - Develop diabetes

° Develop heart disease

° Suffer from a stroke

° Become diagnosed with cancer

° Get one or more sexually transmitted diseases

° Have depression

° Attempt suicide

° Die at an earlier age

- When compared to counterparts who did not endure adverse childhood experiences, children who did are:

  ° 5x more likely to have depression

  ° 7x more likely to be addicted to alcohol

  ° 10x more likely to use or become addicted to drugs

  ° 12x more likely to attempt suicide

The impact of trauma, particularly of chronic and complex trauma, is far reaching. You may be wondering, though, how to recognize children and teens who may have been exposed to trauma, so that you can determine the best approaches for support. Below, you will find "look fors" that typically manifest in children or teens who have been exposed to trauma. These descriptions are meant to provide you with considerations to reflect upon when determining how to best support the needs of children/teens with which you are working. While these "look fors" may indicate exposure to trauma, it is important to note that they may be caused by other unrelated factors such as preexisting learning disabilities, cultural norms, personality, etc. In the next section, we will explore elements of becoming a trauma-informed professional and how to provide the best support for children/teens who have been impacted by trauma or hardship.

SNAPSHOT LOOK FORs

EMOTIONAL

Worry/anxiety

Irritabilities

Aggression/anger

Distrust

Sadness

Hopelessness

Hyper-alertness

Emotional numbness

Mood swings

Guilt or shame

BEHAVIORAL

Lack of recognition of social cues

Clinginess

Difficulty with authority

Difficulty with criticism

Whininess

Appear withdrawn

Outbursts

Avoidance

Absenteeism

PHYSICAL

Tiredness/fatigue

Easily startled

Edginess

Aches and pains

Headaches

Stomach aches

Hunger

Hyperactivity

Hypoactivity

Overreaction to minor injuries

Key Elements of Becoming a Trauma-Informed Professional

Now that you have a strong understanding of trauma and its impact, you may be wondering how you can use this information to help the children and/or teens with whom you work. The next two sections will be devoted to answering these questions by:

1. Investigating what it looks like to be a trauma-informed professional working in a trauma-informed culture of professionals. We will highlight key attributes of research-based models and in current literature that have demonstrated effectiveness when supporting those impacted by trauma. Note that the descriptions in this section are meant to provide basic principles. More information can be found within the resources cited in the Reference section of this guide.

2. Exploring various elements of a trauma-informed environment, as well as techniques and strategies that encourage wellness and resiliency.

The Trauma-Informed Culture

There currently exists ample research-based models on establishing and retaining a trauma-informed culture within your professional community. While these models are built upon differing frames, they are interlaced with common threads of understanding. Cited below are some of the most commonly known models.

The Substance Abuse and Mental Health Services Administration (SAMHSA), an agency within the United States Department of Health and Human Services, has been at the forefront of trauma-informed care. As such, they have identified core components and principles to consider when creating a strong professional support base for those impacted by trauma. These core components and principles include the 4Rs and STPCEC. In short, these acronyms denote:

4Rs

- *Realize* the prevalence of trauma.
- *Recognize* how trauma affects all survivors, stakeholders, professionals, and all others within the specific institution or community.

- *Resist* re-traumatizing survivors.
- *Respond* with the appropriate methods involved in trauma-informed care.

Core Principles

- *Safety:* Ensure the physical and emotional safety of everyone within the organizational community.
- *Trustworthiness:* Ensure clarity of purpose, roles, and boundaries within the organizational community.
- *Peer Support:* Create an environment of support and care within the organizational community.
- *Collaboration and Mutuality:* Prioritize collaboration within the organizational community.
- *Empowerment, Choice, and Control:* Maximize skill building, collaborative decision-making, and utilization of individual skill sets within the organizational community.
- *Cultural, Historical, and Gender Issues:* Recognize, reflect, and move beyond biases and misunderstandings of individuals within the organizational community.

Similar to the SAMHSA model is that of Sandra Bloom's Sanctuary Model. This model, which is dedicated to helping organizations effectively support those who have been impacted by trauma, seems to place a stronger emphasis on building relationships in a manner that paves the path for individualized empowerment of those impacted by trauma. The Sanctuary Model is based on

four pillars of shared: (a) knowledge, (b) values), (c) language of S.E.L.F. (safety, emotions, loss, future), and (d) practice. It implores that trauma-informed organizations make seven commitments to the population with which they serve. These commitments include:

- *Non-Violence:* Strengthen skills related to safety.
- *Emotional Intelligence:* Strengthen skills related to emotional regulation and management.
- *Social Learning:* Build cognitive skills.
- *Open Communication:* Enhance ability to effectively communicate and to establish healthy boundaries.
- *Social Responsibility:* Promote healthy attachments and relationships, build social skills, establish a sense of fairness and justice.
- *Democracy:* Strengthen skills related to self-control and self-discipline.
- *Growth and Change:* Work through trauma and forge ahead with strength, confidence, and hope.

An additional source worth referencing is that of the National Child Traumatic Stress Network (NCTSN). The NCTSN model includes elements to protect the well-being of professionals working with those who have been impacted by trauma, as well as more concrete steps to ensure the safety and well-being of children/teens at all levels of need. This organization has emphasized ten essential elements that they deem necessary in order to create a trauma-informed environment in which children feel safe, supported, and able to flourish.

These elements include:

- identification and assessment of traumatic stress,
- addressing and treatment of traumatic stress,
- trauma education and awareness for stakeholders,
- creation of partnerships with the children or teen and their family,
- creation of an environment that promotes resilience, social-emotional wellness, and overall well-being,
- cultural responsiveness and recognition of how culture can impact support and practice,
- crisis management and a strong plan for emergency response,
- addressing of and attention to compassion fatigue and staff self-care,
- evaluation and revision of institutional policy and practice, and
- cross-systems collaboration and establishment of community partnerships.

A final resource to spotlight is that of the National Center for Biotechnology Information (NCBI), a division of the National Institutes of Health (NIH). This agency contains a great deal of research and information on a number of essential topics as they relate to health and medicine. One in particular, their publication *Trauma-Informed Care in Behavioral Health Services,* provides essential details in creating and sustaining an organizational culture of trauma-informed professionals. A few themes to underscore from

this framework (which can be found at https://www.ncbi.nlm.nih.gov/books/NBK207204/) include:

- trauma awareness and understanding,
- organizational, administrative, and full stakeholder commitment,
- establishment of common values, purpose, and mission,
- ongoing reflection, review, evaluation, and updating of policy and practice to ensure growth and continuous strengthening of care,
- strategic establishment of plans (implementation, follow up, emergency, self-care, etc.),
- clarity of roles, responsibilities, and collaborative and strategic methods,
- safety and support for the team of professional learners,
- collaborative partnerships within the community,
- consistent training and education,
- assessment of and plans of action for specific cases, and
- cultural implications, common issues within services, and how to overcome them to provide the best support.

A trauma-informed culture is one which includes ongoing commitment to the mission and vision, reflection, strategic modification as needed, and one which consistently evaluates systemic practice to ensure evolution in their ability to support all stakeholders within the institution. Safety, engagement, connection, conscious acceptance, and encouragement remain core components of a trauma-informed culture. Methods and practices for establishing and increasing these core components can be found in the *Tips for Presenting to Staff and Supports* section of this guide.

We have just identified quite a few core elements needed to create a trauma-informed culture within your professional community. Next, let's look at some techniques and strategies that you may consider using as a trauma-informed professional. It is important to note that we are providing a basic sense of approaches that have been proven beneficial in the current literature and research. Proper training in these techniques and strategies is highly recommended before putting into practice.

The Trauma-Informed Professional

Now that we have identified research-based structures within a trauma-informed culture, let's examine key features of becoming a trauma-informed professional in a trauma-informed environment. In the figure below, you will find snapshot kernels related to creating an environment conducive to cultivating resilience, as well as best practices when working with children and teens who have faced adversity.

Common Themes and Essentials as Evidenced by Current Literature and Research

Environment

- Awareness, understanding, and ongoing education

- Common mission, values, and vision
- Commitment and communication
- Full stakeholder involvement
- Safety support, empowerment, and commitment to professional growth and self-care
- Ongoing reflection, evaluation, and upgrading of policy and practice
- Clarity of roles and methods
- Collaborative partnerships with colleagues and community
- Social, emotional, and behavioral skill-building
- Cultural implication, biases, and strategic plans for overcoming hindrances to care

Best Practices and Tips

- Relationships:
  - Ensure safety and comfort.
  - Be patient.
  - Avoid assumptions.
  - Create a trusting, supportive, and affirming relationship.
  - Check in consistently. Be visible and available.
  - Get to know families, caretakers, and community.
  - Become attuned – be aware of verbal and non-verbal cues, causes, and be flexible in these moments.
  - Use humor (as appropriate).

- Discipline:
  - ° Establish clear routines and inform the child or teen of any changes ahead of time.
  - ° Offer choices to allow for a sense of control.
  - ° Set clear and firm limits and establish logical consequences (positive and negative, that align with actions, as opposed to punishments and/or praise without purpose).
  - ° Create learning opportunities where the child/teen can take ownership and reflect on ways to repair wrongdoings.
  - ° Avoid power struggles.
  - ° Do not take things personally.
  - ° Avoid excluding actions such as "time-out" or taking away time to engage.
  - ° Manage your reactions and reflect after moments of elevation.
  - ° Acknowledge good choices and desired actions.
  - ° Provide simple and clear feedback.
  - ° Be consistent.
- Academic and Emotional:
  - ° Avoid re-traumatization.
  - ° Strengthen communication, social skills, and emotional intelligence skills (social and self- emotional intelligence).
  - ° Use person-centered techniques and practices.
  - ° Build on strengths and interests, provide constructive praise, and provide confidence-boosting activities.
  - ° Think outside-the-box, get creative, use alternatives modes of support, and do not be afraid to meet the children/teens where they need to be met.

Considerations/Food for Thought:

- The brain is brilliantly resilient and can recover from trauma with the proper attention, tools, care, support, and guidance.
- The whole self has infallible "bouncebackability" and can recover from trauma with the proper attention, tools, care, support, and guidance.
- A trauma-informed/resiliency-strengthening approach to supporting children and teens must include a set of key awarenesses, understandings, and factors in order to be successful.
- Time, patience, consistency, and unwavering dedication and care are crucial.
- Follow the pace of the child or teen and be mindful of neurodevelopmental needs.
- Reinforce new strategies and techniques in order to create new neural pathways.
- A few setbacks are to be expected. Don't give up.

- Be curious about behaviors and cognitions, ask open-ended questions, actively listen, and do not make assumptions.

- Continuously reflect and be extra mindful of your own wellness and how you are being impacted.

Creating an environment that is conducive to resilience-strengthening is critical to the success of children and teens who have been impacted by trauma. The coming sections will explore this idea even further. We will highlight:

- key elements of resiliency,

- techniques for cultivating resilience, and

- strategies to enhance overall wellbeing that are both practical and adaptable based on preferences and developmental needs.

The Brilliantly Resilient Brain: Plasticity

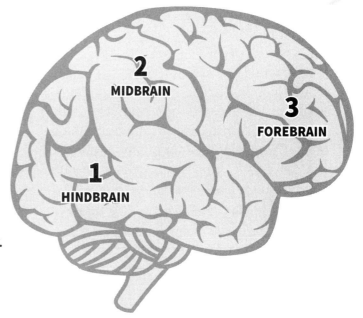

This module focuses on the brain. We will look at parts of the brain and their function, as well as how these parts work together (or fail to work together) in response to trauma. We will then focus on the wondrous plasticity of the human brain. This includes an exploration of the brain's capability to adapt, repair, and heal from trauma. Finally, we will reflect on the concept of resiliency and areas of focus when strengthening resiliency.

Brain 101: A Quick Glance at the Brain and Stress Response

The brain is generally made up of three main parts:

1. the *hindbrain,* which regulates our automatic responses, arousal, and reflexes,

2. the *midbrain,* which, among other things, processes our experiences, emotions, stores memory, and houses the *amygdala* and the *hippocampus,* and

3. the *forebrain,* which houses our higher-order thinking, communication skills, problem-solving skills, and which houses the *hypothalamus.*

Let's take a quick moment to explore stress response. As explained earlier, the midbrain houses the amygdala and the hippocampus. One primary role of the amygdala is that of an alert system, as it is also the storer of fear memories and therefore holds the power of recognizing potential danger. During moments of possible risk, the amygdala, oftentimes along with the help of the hippocampus, sends an alert to the hypothalamus in the forebrain. The hypothalamus then sends messages to the rest of the body, instructing relevant areas to prepare to defend against the threat or perceived threat. The hindbrain reacts in ways that heighten your senses (arousal, increased heart rate and breathing, etc.) to prepare you for action.

Think of a time when you have felt so terrified that your body automatically responded before you had a chance to think. Perhaps you heard a loud noise late at night, fell victim to a goose attack, or encountered some other frightening and unexpected situation. Looking back, did you respond in the best way possible? Do you remember stopping to take stock and to make a sage decision? Most likely, you acted on instinct. Those primal intuitions kicked in, the fight or flight mode was activated, and your body reacted before you could even process what was going on.

To achieve our optimal selves, we need these major parts of our brains to work together in a united alliance. Imagine your brain is your favorite football team.

- Consider your forebrain as the coach: filled with the wisdom and experience necessary to make the best choices and to create a killer playbook of genius action plans.
- The QB is the midbrain: soaking up the environment around him, using his previous knowledge, and going with what he feels in the moment to determine the best play given the context of the situation.
- The rest of the offensive and defensive lines make up the other vital players involved with fear response: doing what they need to do to protect the ball and to get the win.
- The hindbrain is the overall energy flowing through the players: the rush that causes elevated heart rate and breathing so they can feel powerful enough to move mountains, the gusto that allows them to instinctively put their hands up when the ball is hurling towards them, or to move when an opposing player is hurling their body at them.

When the players are warmed up, attuned to each other, and functioning like a well-oiled machine, stellar plays are made and those ever-treasured touchdowns are inevitable. However, if the defensive ends are down for the count or the quarterback pulls a hammy, then we blindly toss Hail Mary passes and race around like a ship without a rudder.

Ideally, all parts of the brain should work together in one powerful synergistic manner. During a stressful situation, though, that may not happen as the midbrain reacts before the forebrain can process and determine the best action plan. Like when the QB tosses an interception because a lineman slipped, allowing for a few opposing players to come barreling towards him. Stress and fear can hinder brain performance in this way. During stressful events, major players within the brain may find themselves unable to work as a cohesive unit, to communicate with each other effectively, and to determine the best plan of action together.

Now, imagine the long-term impact that chronic fear and constant stress can

have on the brain. Moreover, imagine the impact on a brain that is still developing. Complex trauma is a hurdle that could severely and permanently impact flow and brain performance.

However...

Just as trauma can negatively impact the brain, research has shown that these effects can be reversed!

Consider your phone. I'm sure you have felt the frustration of seeing that almost ever-present red "update" reminder floating over the settings icon. Our phones are constantly upgrading and reconfiguring. When new demands arise (who doesn't love expanding on their emoji library or gaining the ability to simultaneously filter selfies, talk to a friend, order dinner delivery, monitor heart rate, and check emails?) or when glitches and bugs in current phone offerings present themselves, our trusty handheld assistants are on top of it – enhancing abilities and modifying current networks to provide us with the latest and greatest!

Just as our phones have the ability to upgrade, enhance themselves, and to fix glitches and errors in the system, our brains (with the proper supports and circumstances) have the unbelievable ability to reconfigure, to adapt, repair glitches or bugs, and enhance overall performance.

How?

Plasticity: What Is it?

You most likely have heard terms such as flexibility, pliability, or elasticity in recent discussions or training. Brain plasticity, or neuroplasticity, refers to the brain's ability to adapt and modify in response to the environment. This astounding ability to overcome and to heal can be likened to a starfish. Whereas a starfish can regenerate and heal from lost limbs, so can the brain rebuild and repair faulty pathways.

Research has indicated that neurological damage done by trauma can be reversed due to the brain's resiliency and, you guessed it, its flexibility, pliability, and elasticity.

Current studies show great promise in expanding upon this understanding. Leitch (2017) explains that neuroplasticity can aid in strengthening overall wellness and prosocial behaviors via skill-building and self-directed development.

Ready for a high school throwback?

"Neurons that fire together, wire together; neurons that fire apart, wire apart."

This catchy phrase helps to explain neuroplasticity and trauma. Our brains create neural pathways when they fire simultaneously and consistently together. A set of synapses eventually cruises on autopilot down this pathway, allowing us to maintain certain understandings or to complete specific actions without much effort. Like your favorite cup of coffee. It may have taken some exploration to determine the perfect roast and amount of cream and sugar that suits your taste but once you got it down, you could brew up a perfect cup with your eyes closed. Due to neuroplasticity, your brain has adapted and rewired itself to allow you this personal-taste barista skill.

While this idea applies to the maladaptive thoughts and behaviors that are created by trauma, it also applies to the brain's ability to rewire and repair these faulty neural pathways. Consistent exposure and experience with the proper skills development, thought patterns, environment, and support system, can lead to an override of faulty pathways in favor of new and healthy ones.

The Infallible "Bouncebackable" Self: Resiliency

Resiliency is generally understood to be the learned skill or ability to overcome challenges or life-altering events and experiences, as well as the ability to grow and to strengthen one's self in the aftermath of such an event or experience. Psychologist and author Dr. Rick Hanson elaborates on this by explaining that resilience requires meeting the basic needs of safety, satisfaction, and connection through responsive means (Hanson & Hanson, 2018). According to the American Psychological Association (2020), strengthening one's resilience takes time and purposeful attention to the four areas of: connection, wellness, healthy thinking, and meaning making. Moreover, Hanson (2018) postulates that resilience can be strengthened by: (a) finding healthy ways to increase positive and beneficial resources (which relates to connections), (b) establishing safeguards in times of vulnerability (which relates to wellness), and (c) seeking new opportunities, confronting challenges, and managing setbacks in a constructive manner (which relates to healthy thinking and meaning making).

In order to combat negative thought patterns and stress-related issues that

come with trauma, Dr. William Bridges (1980) suggests that focus be placed on strengthening the four Cs that most fear losing in times of trauma. Those four Cs are: *control, choice, competence,* and *connection.* Focus on strengthening these areas may lead to a more positive outcome and post-traumatic growth. In the next section, *Snap Skills: Resilience-Strengthening,* we will explore possible ways to ensure that the four C's are met when working with children and/or teens who have been impacted by trauma.

Tedeschi, Park, and Calhoun (1998) coined the term "post-traumatic growth" (PTG) as a means of describing a positive psychological change that happens in the aftermath of trauma, which results in a new understanding of and a greater appreciation for life, a new perspective of pain, and the ability to channel pain in a productive manner. Tedeschi and colleagues further explain that PTG can be reflected in positive shifts such as: facing fears and embracing new opportunities, heightened spirituality, a greater appreciation of life, improved relationships, greater pleasures in daily happenings, and emotional growth.

Additionally, an organization dedicated to stopping the stigmas related to mental illness See Me Scotland, has outlined core areas of focus when seeking to increase resilience. These areas include:

- *Self-Awareness and Acceptance:* Appreciate self, maintain self-love, confidence, and self-worth; accept positive praise, and recognize the value of self.

- *Connection:* Maintain positive and healthy relationships with trusted

SNAPSHOT: THEMES SURROUNDING RESILIENCE-STRENGTHENING

APA's components of resiliency	Charney's characteristics that cultivate resiliency	Hanson's resiliency areas of focus	Bridge's four areas of focus	See Me Scotland's core areas of focus
Connection	• Generosity • Desire to help others • Positive and encouraging support network	• Seek and maintain positive and nurturing relationships • Engage in acts of kindness • Help others	Connection	Connection and contribution
Wellness	• Humor	• Create goals and actively take steps to reach them • Increase courage and grit • Strengthen confidence • Practice calm and balance	Control	Self-Awareness
Healthy Thinking	• Moral compass • Optimism • Facing fears	• Focus on the positives • Practice gratitude • Embrace the present • Create an internal locus of control • Develop a sense of agency	Competence	Health
Meaning Making	• Faith • Embracing new challenges • Desire to learn • Opportunity seeking	• Knowledge seeking • Experience seeking • Cultivating grit • Seek opportunities for growth • Embrace challenges	Choice	Acceptance

friends, family, community, and surround yourself with those who recognize and appreciate your value.

- *Contribution:* Become involved in something bigger than self, volunteer, and channel passions and skills towards helping the greater good.
- *Health:* Maintain proper physical, emotional, mental, and overall wellness and hygiene habits.

With the proper tools, mindset, and support, children and teens who have been impacted by trauma can come out not only accepting of the event(s), but stronger as a result. When seeking to cultivate resilience and encourage post-traumatic growth, it is important to focus on the core areas related to strengthening overall ability to overcome, and to seek opportunity in, challenges. The resources described in this chapter have highlighted such areas of focus. Common themes among current literature related to cultivating resiliency and encouraging post-traumatic growth generally lie around:

- understanding self (confidence, awareness, acceptance),
- social strengths (trusted and positive support networks, working towards something bigger than self), and
- internal strengths (grit, meaning making, embracing new opportunities for growth, personal points of wellness, positive mindset).

In the next section, we will explore specific techniques used to cultivate and strengthen resilience.

Snap Skills: Resilience-Strengthening

In the previous module, we explored plasticity and the brain's magnificent ability to heal from trauma. This module is dedicated to distinguishing the various elements that make up resiliency. Various tools, techniques, and strategies that may be used to strengthen resiliency in children and adolescents will also be examined. The module ends with considerations to reflect on when determining individualized resiliency plans.

Research suggests that resiliency is not a trait, but rather a learned skill. As such, the "snap skills" identified in this section are meant to strengthen and increase resiliency.

Zone of Resiliency	Activities that Increase this Zone of Resiliency
Self-Acceptance	<ul><li>Create and use mantras</li><li>Explore positive journaling</li><li>Plan strengths-based activities</li><li>Create time for growth mindset activities (see *Reference* page for more information on Carol Dweck's *Mindsets*)</li><li>Recommend goal-setting and progress-tracking</li><li>Create confidence-boosting activities</li><li>Create positive team-building and collaborative activities</li><li>Promote daily positive self-talk prompts</li><li>Make time for opportunities to promote social skills</li><li>Make time for emotional intelligence-strengthening activities</li></ul>
Self-Awareness	<ul><li>Promote daily gratitude activities</li><li>Model mindfulness moments</li><li>Explore time for body-scanning</li><li>Create a daily mood and thoughts tracker</li><li>Practice grounding techniques</li><li>Practice titillation and pendulation</li></ul>

Zone of Resiliency	Activities that Increase this Zone of Resiliency
Contribution	<ul><li>Volunteer</li><li>Use talents and passions to help others</li><li>Mentor (even young children can be tasked to teach and guide peers)</li><li>Establish roles and responsibilities that lead to confidence and knowledge that one helped the greater good</li><li>Promote "good citizen" actions</li><li>Discuss values, morals, and how to make good choices</li></ul>
Connection	<ul><li>Promote positive interactions and teamwork</li><li>Invite children/teens to join clubs, teams, organizations, and other social structures that promote positivity</li><li>Write letters, cards, emails, texts, or call trusted and supportive loved ones</li><li>Work out in the community</li></ul>
Health	<ul><li>Physical<ul><li>Establish healthy eating habits</li><li>Create fun and achievable exercise plans</li><li>Ensure daily movement</li><li>Promote morning and evening stretches</li></ul></li><li>Mental/Emotional<ul><li>Explore relaxation and regulation strategies</li><li>Explore pampering/self-care strategies</li><li>Establish self-care routines</li><li>Ensure time to explore hobbies and passions</li><li>Allow for a positive role model to be present</li><li>Make time for leisure and socializing</li><li>Promote humor, laughing, and flexibility</li><li>Focus on effort as opposed to perfection</li><li>Encourage challenging negative self-talk with positive self-talk</li></ul></li><li>Hygiene<ul><li>Create a daily routine</li><li>Establish good sleep habits</li><li>Establish daily self-cleansing habits</li></ul></li></ul>
Grit	<ul><li>Set goals and track progress</li><li>Have a sense of purpose</li><li>Teach self-regulation skills</li><li>Take positive risks and get outside of comfort zone (in a positive and safe manner that leads to a productive outcome)</li><li>Seek new experiences and opportunities</li><li>Explore new skills, new learnings, and growth</li><li>Cultivate an optimistic and future-forward mindset</li></ul>

The table on the previous page identifies various areas, or "zones" connected to resiliency. Each "zone" is identified on the left-hand column. The corresponding activities and exercises associated with strengthening these zones are located in the right-hand column directly across. These activities and exercises are not exhaustive, but are meant to serve as examples and guides that can be expanded upon.

A further source to consider when providing trauma-recovery and resilience-skills as a trauma-informed professional is the Trauma Resiliency Model (TRM). This somatic-focused approach is geared towards mental health professionals. TRM emphasizes nine skills that are believed to be helpful in: (a) stabilizing the nervous system, (b) decreasing the effects of traumatic stress, and (c) supporting healthy processing and reflection of traumatic experiences (Grabbe, L. & Miller-Karas, E., 2018). These nine skills are comprised of:

- *Tracking:* Guide the youth through active reflection on feelings (physical and emotional) during times of stress and times of calm. This allows for them to monitor, process, and distinguish between the two extremes.

- *Resourcing and Resource Intensification:* Ask the youth to identify one source of comfort and safety (a person, place, item, activity, etc.). Expand on this by asking descriptive and sensory-provoking questions to allow for the creation of positive neural pathways to counter negative feelings and emotions. The addition of resiliency-focused questions that focus on inner strengths and grit, increase the impact of this skill.

- *Grounding:* Focusing on the present moment, calming physical sensations, sensory and tangible environmental objects, etc. can be used not only to distract from negative thoughts or emotions, but also to create a sense of safety and control. For more information on grounding techniques, refer to the "Snap Skills" section of this toolkit.

- *Gesturing:* Mirroring open soothing gestures and recognition of the accompanying feelings can be self-soothing and can strengthen self-regulation. Gesturing involves this action: slow and repetitive mirroring of such actions.

- *Help Now!:* The "Help Now!" skill includes 10 strategies that distract from present stress due to trauma or triggered emotions. Samples of these skills can be found in the "Snap Skills" section of this toolkit.

- *Shift and Stay:* This skill asks the youth to reflect on and to become consciously aware of their symptoms when triggered (physical, emotional). When this awareness is evident, they can then make a choice as to which coping technique would diminish the symptoms.

- *Titration:* This skill involves asking the youth to be consciously aware of smaller and more manageable sensations that arise when triggered. This allows the small piece to be concretized (describe this feeling's weight, shape, size) and eventually diminished.

- *Pendulation:* In this skill, the child or teen is encouraged to reflect and become aware of physical and emotional sensations during times of stress and times of calm. By swaying back and forth between these two, a clear understanding of the balance point is reached.

- *Completion of Survival Response:* This skill allows for closure to a traumatic event, as it asks the youth to act out the proper or desired defensive response that they may not have had the chance to complete during the traumatic event due to brain and body reactivity.

Additionally, the International Resiliency Project, a research study which spanned across 11 countries, found three instrumental sources from which children can draw resilience. These include:

- *"I have" sources:* Present external supports and resources that encourage and strengthen resilience

- *"I am" sources:* Internal qualities (feelings, attitudes, beliefs) that cultivate resilience

- *"I can" sources:* Social and interpersonal skills

(Yates and Masten, 2012)

Providing opportunities to identify these sources, as well as opportunities to brainstorm how to use them, could prove beneficial in terms of strengthening resilience. This can be done through one-on-one or group discussions and activities, as well as through solitary activities such as prompted journaling or art.

Considerations/Food for Thought

When determining how to engage children/teens in activities related to overcoming trauma, consider the following:

- Personality, traits, and abilities
- Comfort and safety
- Developmental level
- Ensuring that you touch on each of the "zones" identified above
- Your personal strengths, skill sets, and qualifications

Snap Skills: Strategies and Techniques

This module of "snap skills" will explore a broad scope of tools that may be useful when strengthening resiliency in children and adolescents. A comprehensive list of strategies and techniques separated by purpose will be explored, followed by a more in-depth look at what these strategies and techniques involve (purpose and procedure). Considerations for more individualized needs, as well as general reflections when determining which tools to use, will be discussed.

The "snap skills" identified below are universal tools that can be used anywhere, anytime. They are exploratory in nature and meant to be sampled in a "trial-and-error" approach in order to determine which skills are most favorable and helpful for the individual child or teen.

A few tips to remember:

- Each "snap skill" serves a unique purpose. The table headings indicate general objectives to guide you in your determination of which "snap skill" may be most useful at a given time. Keep in mind that, while they may be housed under one heading, many of these skills overlap into other areas, as well.

- An *asterisk next to the "snap skill" indicates that further information on that skill will follow. Please refer to the "Snap Skills Snapshots" notes under the table to learn more about these skills.

- These "snap skills" meet a broadbrush of whole-body-and-mind needs. Each particular sample is geared towards specific areas of these needs and is meant to enhance one or more of the following:
  ◦ processing
  ◦ release of energy
  ◦ grounding
  ◦ calming
  ◦ positivity
  ◦ confidence
  ◦ increase of focus
  ◦ alleviation of negative feelings
  ◦ anxiety reduction

- Additionally, these "snap skills" touch on a broad array of strengths, preferences, and styles, in order to promote enjoyable sampling and determination of skills that are best suited for each personality. Some of the strengths, preferences, and styles explored include:

- ○ movement/physical
- ○ oral/social focus
- ○ written
- ○ musical/auditory
- ○ visual arts
- ○ intrapersonal focus
- ○ focus on others, nature, and social pieces

- Remember that this is a comprehensive list. Take your time exploring them, perhaps choosing 1-3 as needed. Be sure to reflect after sampling, make note of those that are most beneficial, and use that knowledge to create a personalized action plan.

Release of Energy	Processing	Focus/Grounding/Calming
• *Scratch art • *Wall pushes • *Progressive muscle relaxation (PMR) • Rip paper • Chew on something crunchy such as carrot sticks or apples • Squeeze clay, slime, etc. • Jump rope • Play ball, run, paintball, get out and move • Punch or scream into a pillow • Sing as loud as your can along with a fun, fast, loud song	• *Draw your emotions • *Color your emotions • *Channel your emotions with various artforms • *Write a letter • *Body scan • *Emotions scan/decomposing of • Listen to songs that resonate with you • Create a puppet show • Draw a cartoon about the experience • Scribble art • Write a song or poem • Journal • Talk with someone who you trust • Purposeful use of bibliotherapy and reflective discussion of the story	• *Mandala or zentangle drawings • *Purposeful breathing • *Pendulate • *Sensory exploration • Sniff comforting scents • Touch a variety of materials (stuffed toys, velcro, ice, heated blanket, etc.) • Pay attention to your body and the points at which it hits the floor, chair, etc. • Listen to low tones, rhythms, sounds, vibrations • Stretch your body • Practice yoga or a light movement exercise • Run your hands under alternating cool and warm water • Chew mint gum • Play "I-Spy"

Confidence/Positivity	Anxiety Reduction	Release of Negative Feelings
<ul><li>*Tapping/EFT</li><li>*Tell yourself a mantra</li><li>Create something</li><li>Bake or cook</li><li>Dance</li><li>Create a vision board</li><li>Write your goals down and how you will reach them</li><li>Write down things that you are grateful for</li><li>Shift your perspective and consider the positives</li><li>Put on your favorite outfit</li><li>Take pictures in nature or of positive images</li><li>Put scented lotion on your hands and focus on the smell, the texture, the feeling</li></ul>	<ul><li>*Reflexology</li><li>*Imagery</li><li>*Practice Jin Shin Jyutsu hand pressure</li><li>*Challenge negative thoughts</li><li>Hug yourself</li><li>Guided visualization</li><li>Hold your own hands and comfort yourself</li><li>Stroke your chest bone or rub your ears</li><li>Gently apply pressure to your temples, your nose bridge, and to the back of your head with your fingers</li><li>Use a handheld head or back massager</li><li>Watch your favorite show or read your favorite blog</li><li>Play a brain teaser game</li><li>Gently roll your feet back and forth over a tennis ball</li></ul>	<ul><li>*Laugh</li><li>*Hand-over-heart self-love</li><li>Call a friend</li><li>Exercise</li><li>Go out with a friend</li><li>Go for a walk</li><li>Volunteer</li><li>Perform a small act of kindness</li><li>Determine what is in your control and use this to move forward</li><li>Accept</li><li>Do something goofy</li><li>Try a new skill (dance, cooking, painting, woodwork, acting, etc.)</li><li>Change your environment – take a walk, go to another room, go somewhere to recharge</li></ul>

SNAP SKILLS SNAPSHOTS

Release of Energy

- *Scratch art:*

  Using a pencil or pen, scribble on a piece of paper as quick and as hard as you can.
- *Wall pushes:*

  Stand with your arms extended and hands pressed against a wall. Push as hard as you can, as if you are trying to move the wall.
- *Progressive muscle relaxation (PMR):*

  Focusing on specific parts of the body at a time, tense and squeeze as you inhale deeply. Hold your breath for 5 counts while still tensing this part of your body, then gently release that tension as you exhale. Repeat 3x before moving on to the next part of your body. Try this process with your legs, feet, hands, arms, and stomach.

Processing

- *Draw your emotions:*

  Draw a picture, abstract or with true-to-life forms, to express your emotions.
- *Color your emotions:*

  Use colors to express what you are feeling. You can use many colors in various shapes and sizes to illustrate how much or how little you are feeling the emotion, or any other creative thought that pops into your head about use of color.
- *Channel your emotions with various art forms:*

  Create visual art using a variety of materials. Play musical instruments. Move your body to express how you feel. Write a story, play, song, or poem. Act. Use your imagination, creativity, and let go of any feelings of judgement or needs for perfectionism. Let yourself go and create.
- *Write a letter:*

  To yourself (past, present, future), to someone who hurt you, to someone you admire. Write a letter expressing your feelings. Do not send it. Just get the feelings out of your body and directed towards someone with whom you have something to say.
- *Body scan:*

  Get in touch with how your body aligns with your feelings. Check in with each part of your body by focusing on their sensations one at a time (arms, legs, knees, feet, hands, neck, back, head, stomach). Reflect on what you are feeling in each.
- *Emotions scan/decomposing of:*

  We often feel more than one emotion at a time. Take a moment to decompose your feelings. Pull them out, one at a time, and reflect on each emotion that you are feeling one by one.

Confidence/Positivity

- *Tell yourself a mantra:*

  A mantra is like a personal mood/confidence-boosting slogan. Think of a short, simple sentence and repeat it to yourself over and over. This eventually becomes ingrained in your brain and allows you to find the strength to move forward with confidence and positivity.

- *Tapping/EFT:*

  Almost like acupuncture without needles, tapping, or EFT, requires you to simultaneously:

  - Focus your mental energy on a negative feeling in the moment (worry, anxiety, anger).

  - Repeatedly tell yourself a mantra in which you accept the feeling and remind yourself that you are going to get through it, such as, "Even though I am feeling_____, I fully and deeply accept myself," or, "I may feel _____ right now, but, I am strong and will get through this."

  - Gently tap the 9 energy, or meridian, points on your body 5-10 times with 2-4 fingers.

  The energy points to tap include:

  - top of your head
  - inner corner of your eyebrows/the top of your nose bridge
  - temples
  - under your eyes, right above your cheekbones
  - under your nose/your upper lip
  - chin
  - collarbone
  - under your armpits (cross your arms over your chest to reach both sides at once)
  - the heel of your hand, or, the "karate chop" area

Anxiety Reduction

- *Reflexology:*

  Similar to EFT/tapping, reflexology involves placing gentle pressure on energy points on your hands and feet. Gently press and rub each toe, sides, ball, heel, and bottom center of your foot to alleviate minor bodily pain, anxiety, worry, and negative emotions. Experiment with various pressures and points on your feet and hands, if desired. Pay attention to how activating these pressure points makes you feel emotionally, in terms of pains such as headaches, etc.

- *Imagery:*

  Go on a mini-mind vacation. Create pictures in your mind. Imagine you are in a place that makes you feel warm, safe, happy. Use your senses to really feel as if you are there. Stay in this mini-mind vacation space as long as you need.

- *Practice Jin Shin Jyutsu hand pressure:*

  An ancient Japanese healing and wellness technique, Jin Shin Jyutsu can be done anywhere at any time. It involves gently massaging and putting pressure/rolling specific fingers with your opposite hand, as each holds the key to a specific feeling or emotion. Doing so will activate your inner power and ability to ease the negative feelings. To start, breathe deeply and concentrate on the present. Massage, roll, and apply pressure to your fingers as indicated below:

  - ☐ Pinky-Low confidence, self-doubt, unsure about self
  - ☐ Ring-Anxiety, worry, edginess
  - ☐ Middle-Anger, frustration, resentment
  - ☐ Index-Terror, fear, feeling afraid or panicked
  - ☐ Thumb-Sadness, grief, hopelessness

  (Retrieved from: https://www.jinshininstitute.com/)

- *Challenge negative thoughts:*

  When the negative or unhelpful thoughts pop up, step up to them with questions like:

  1. What proof do I have that this is true?
  2. What are some other ways of looking at this?
  3. What would I tell a friend who was thinking this way?
  4. Will this matter to me in a month?

Release of Negative Feelings

- *Laugh:*

    Challenge yourself to find something that gives you the biggest belly chuckle. Check out some memes or GIFs, watch a funny YouTube clip, read a funny blog, listen to a funny podcast, read "dad jokes" or a joke book, watch funny animal acts online, do what it takes to laugh until your eyes water up and your stomach hurts.

- *Hand-over-heart self-love:*

    When feeling low, sometimes the best thing is a warm, heartfelt touch. That is where the hand-over-heart self-love skill comes in! Place one hand over your heart and the other hand on your stomach. Slowly breathe in and out, feeling the warmth and energy from your hands as they cradle your heart and stomach. Focus on this energy flow as you continue to breathe purposefully. It may enhance the feelings if you close your eyes or if you repeat positive thoughts in your head (e.g., "I am strong," "I am brave," "I am loved," "I am worthy."). You may wish to alternate hands to see if this increases the positive energy flow.

PART 2
Leadership-
Focused Resource

Leadership-Focused Resource

Designed primarily for school, mental health, and community leaders, this section will focus on how to train and educate others in trauma and resiliency.

First, we will explore best practices for providing exceptional and enduring professional development (PD). We will then examine relevant fundamental topics and talking points to consider when creating a plan for trauma-informed, resiliency-based professional development. Supplemental activities to enhance the PD experience will also be included in this discussion. The section will conclude by shining a light on compassion fatigue. We will identify indicators of compassion fatigue, as well as approaches to combat it.

The aim of this section is to provide the essential components of quality professional development in order to effectively and efficiently deliver the information shared in the first section of this guide in a manner that demonstrates empathy for your audience. However, the fundamentals provided in this section are applicable to most professional development or training endeavors in general. As such, it is our hope that the information gained in this section can be streamlined to meet your specific needs in future PD ambitions.

Tips for Presenting to Staff and Supports

This module focuses on the elements that make up a solid professional development plan. We will identify and analyze seven key factors that create coherent and productive PD. Included in this analysis are suggestions and guidelines to ensure your professional development plan reaches maximum potential with minimal challenges.

In order to create a successful community of trauma-informed educators, counselors and therapists, or others who support children, leaders must consider the following when providing professional development:

1. Foundational elements of success
2. Setting the tone
3. Purpose, vision, and outcome aspirations
4. Understanding the audience
5. Translating new learning into the classroom or office
6. Home, school, and community relations
7. Monitoring, continuing collaboration and discourse, independent learning, and ongoing engagement

and support through distributed leadership.

1. Foundational Elements of Success

The successful implementation of professional development training on topics that may cause participant discomfort is determinant on a number of factors. While such factors will be discussed in detail further into this guide, some foundational pieces to consider in the initial stages of planning include:

Buy-In:

Staff buy-in is vital in the effort to create a trauma-informed school. Universally, full buy-in can be difficult when dealing with the varying personalities, personal matters, professional burnout, and other individual constructs that occur within teams. Added to this are the uniquely personal feelings that arise when dealing with a hard-hitting topic such as trauma. Staff must recognize how their own experiences and beliefs about trauma impact their ability to take in new information, to appropriately support children who have been impacted by trauma, and to filter through personal biases or misconceptions in order to best meet the needs of their children.

Employing a distributed leadership approach to professional development in which participants feel as partners and take ownership of the acquisition of new knowledge could result in a greater sense of agency, and a more successful outcome overall (Rake et al., 2017). This can be done in part by including participants in all phases of PD, from vision and purpose, to evaluation and follow up, in a way that allows them to draw on their strengths for the good of the whole, while also allowing them to individualize the application of new knowledge in a way that suits their needs.

In order to increase buy-in, leaders must also consider the focus points outlined in the following pages.

Safety and Trust:

Active engagement in a topic that may create discomfort or distress requires a great deal of trust and willingness to step outside of one's comfort zone. Otherwise, people may shut down or shut out information being presented as a means of self-preservation.

Before staff will consider opening themselves up in ways that may make them feel vulnerable (such as actively participating in courageous conversations, taking in new information and using it in a way that alters their practice, or even just the act of learning more about a subject as sensitive as trauma and their students), they must fully trust and

feel safe to do so in their community of colleagues. Leaders must make the effort to set this foundation for staff in order to create a unified sense of safety, trust, and willingness to let guards down.

Time:

Consider the distribution of purpose-driven time both during and in between professional development training, as well as the time allocated for and the time allocated during post-training refreshers. Staff will need ample time to process the information, to critically reflect (self and group), to debrief, to make personal connections, and to own this new understanding of trauma.

Consistent and Targeted Training and Support:

Once a common vision and goals have been established and those initial phases of PD have been completed, there often is a feeling of "We did it! Check that box off and move on." With endless topics, limited time, and constant change within systems, it is easy to let critical elements of PD, such as ongoing monitoring, evaluation, and determination of next steps towards continuous improvement, slide. In order to avoid this circumstance, it is imperative that a PD framework which ensures implementation fidelity and contextual integrity be applied.

One such model, the PrimeD framework, employs four phases (design and development, implementation, evaluation, and research), each designed to interweave and circulate, and to ensure partnership, ownership, and continuous improvement. The PrimeD framework encourages inquiry as a means to determine next steps, allows for strategic and explicit adaptation to contexts and situations, and is framed in a manner that necessitates cyclical engagement and improvement (Rakes et al., 2017).

Reflection:

Reflection through multiple modes is imperative in providing staff with the tools and means necessary for processing, assimilating, accessing, and implementing trauma-informed practices into their pedagogy. Professional development therefore must include frequent and ample time for:

- Critical group and self-reflection
- Group discussions and courageous conversations
- Probing prompts or ideas
- A means to reflect in between and post-professional development training (prompts for flexible personal reflection, a common online community thread, etc.)

Administrator/Leader and Stakeholder Support:

Administrators must not only provide the time and space for professional development, they must also be:

- Present and active participants throughout the professional development process,
- Active in creating enthusiasm and drive for implementing the pieces needed for a trauma-informed environment,
- Cheerleaders in highlighting trauma-informed practices observed beyond the time of professional development training,
- Continuously monitoring and analyzing data to determine next steps in providing what their staff needs to develop mastery in trauma-informed practice,
- Role models in utilizing trauma-informed practices and critical reflection in their daily work, and
- Working towards continuous and productive partnerships between school/office, home, and community.

While these pieces create the foundation for successful implementation of trauma-informed professional development, the components outlined below are key in providing consistent, ongoing, and effective professional development training that staff will carry with them.

2. Setting the tone:

Creating an environment where participants feel safe in opening themselves up to sharing and learning, even when confronted with uncomfortable topics, can be a daunting task. For this reason, as well as for reasons such as time limitations and the desire to be succinct in professional development training, this step is often overlooked. However, it is imperative to set the tone and to create a space where the community of professional learners can fully benefit from the information provided to them.

How do we do this?

In order to set this tone, leaders must consider the audience (more on this to come). They must recognize the various backgrounds, experiences, personalities, and dynamics of their team in order to find common ground and to create a space that is conducive to this kind of personal and professional growth.

Some ideas for setting the tone may include:

- Begin with a clear and authentic conversation. Welcome discussions about what can be done in order to create a secure and non judgmental environment, provide time to share what to do if participants are uncomfortable and need a break, and create a set of mutually agreed upon ground rules.

- Include icebreakers or other amusing activities that allow the team to recognize their own diverse interpersonal quotients, as well as time afterwards to reflect on how they can use this knowledge of self and team to create synergy together and to gain the most from the training.

- Provide quick lessons in critical self and group reflection, in how to constructively debrief, and in how to maintain an open mind and allow other perspectives in.

- Allow time for lightheartedness. Set a theme and provide treats, give staff frequent time to decompress and move, add memes and jokes that keep staff alert and that provide the opportunity to step out of the moment and recharge.

- Understand the concept of change resilience and create an environment that meets staff needs in terms of embracing this new way of thinking and practicing. This can be done through exercises such as:

  ° appreciative inquiry, including:
    - collaborative analysis of current strengths (individual, community, strategies, and approaches) that are successfully supporting children and teens,
    - envisioning what could be if these elements were combined with new trauma-informed practices,
    - collaborative planning based on these combining factors, and
    - implementation and evaluation of these new plans;
  ° individual reflection on personal control and sense of agency in shifting to a more trauma-informed practice;
  ° taking the time to understand where individual hesitation or resilience comes from, and using this understanding to coach/support staff through the process;
  ° trust-building and team-building; and
  ° leadership being present, available, open to communication, and actively involved.

3. Purpose, Vision, and Outcome Aspirations:

A successful professional development plan must include the establishment of an unambiguous purpose, a common vision, and of outcome aspirations. These elements must be clearly stated from the beginning of PD and must be intertwined throughout. They may be used as an introduction or reflection point at the start or end of PD sessions, and should be revisited as reminders during PD activities and beyond the training.

Purpose:

Establishing a clear purpose or mission allows participants to understand specifically what they are learning and why. While this may sound elementary, it is essential in creating community and connection, in defining values, and in creating the building blocks for a common vision and outcome aspirations or goals. Some points to consider when creating the purpose may include:

- Who is your intended audience? What are their roles and what is the setting in which you would like them to utilize this information?

- What are your goals for PD? What do you want the participants to walk away with?

- Why do you want them to walk away with this knowledge?

- Who will the audience be serving with this knowledge?

Vision:

Creating a vision goes hand in hand with the purpose and is essential in establishing a successful community of professional learners. Once the purpose or mission has been established, a common vision can then guide the pathway to reach outcome aspirations, increase availability and buy-in, can create a common connection and desire to work together, and allows participants to hone in and focus on short and long-term goals, as

well as focus and define their role in reaching this goal. In addition to a common vision, participants may also be encouraged to establish their own personal vision that aligns with the community vision. This allows for individualized ownership of the vision, and for personalized accountability and desire to make changes and to continuously improve on practice and pedagogy based on individual strengths, needs, and goals.

Outcome Aspirations:

"Ok, I'm here. I'm at your PD. I understand why I am here and what we hope to create from this but, what's the end goal?"

If participants do not have an end goal in mind, and do not understand the intended outcomes and how the PD will impact them, the community, or those with whom they work, they will not fully buy-in. The purpose and vision may be understood, but, unless they see the forest for the trees, they will not have the motivation to give their all and to fully open themselves up to learning. It is therefore important to clearly define goals of the PD, and to frequently revisit these goals throughout PD sessions. At the beginning and end of each session, it would be useful to clearly explain what the goals of each session are and how they will impact work with children and teens, and then to go back at the end and explain what the goals were, if they were met, and how they resonate with the overarching goals/intended outcomes of the PD in general.

A few points to remember:

- Keep these elements simple, clear, and user-friendly.

- Use common language throughout each of these elements and use this language throughout the PD sessions.

- Encourage participants to take part in active reflection of the purpose, vision, and outcome aspirations throughout the PD and beyond.

- Encourage participants to reflect on their personal vision and goals in terms of this PD, to continuously reflect on how their pedagogy and styles align with their individual and the community vision and goals, and how they can continuously improve and strengthen their practice in order to keep their vision in mind and to reach their outcome aspirations.

Understanding the audience:

As stated earlier, staff buy-in is vital to the success of trauma-informed PD. Understanding your target audience and crafting PD to their needs will greatly increase the odds of gaining full buy-in, inquiry and inspiration to learn, and follow through. According to Osofky (2005), there are four core concepts to consider when planning PD. These concepts are: (1) individual assumptions influence interactions, (2) successful PD is contingent upon shared assumptions and perspectives, (3) emotions influence perceptions and the ability to understand the perspectives of others, and (4) ample time for processing and reflection is critical.

In addition to the guidance provided in this section, a few questions to consider that may help you to better understand your audience include:

General questions to consider:

- Which mindset does each participant tend to lean more towards (growth or fixed)?

- What type of learner is each participant (consider theories such as Garner's Multiple Intelligence, Kolb's Learning Styles, and personal preferences and needs in terms of process time, critical reflection components, comfort in working alone versus with groups, etc.)?

- What schemas are each participant presently working with? What background knowledge do they have? What are their perceptions of the topic and of their comfort-level within the topic? What misperceptions may they have?

- How does individual culture and experience impact understanding, motivation to learn, and perspective on this topic/training in general?

- What individual and/or systemic barriers may be in place that could possibly hinder PD outcomes?

- Do participants feel they have a valued and critical voice/role in this PD, the common vision, and in the outcomes?

- Do participants feel they are in a safe climate and amongst a trusted cohort of professional learners who value their role and thoughts?

- Are participants well-versed in critical peer- and self-reflection and in respectful collaborative discourse?

- Do participants feel that the information is reliable, meaningful, useful in their particular context, and aligns with their professional vision?

- Do participants have a sense of shared ownership and responsibility towards the mission and vision that encapsulates this PD?

Topic-specific questions to consider:

- What background experience does each participant have with trauma-informed practice?
- What previous coursework or training has each participant had with trauma-informed practice?
- Has any participant experienced, or has a loved one experienced, trauma?
- What misconceptions, misperceptions, or biases may each participant presently hold? How can these pieces be addressed?

Translating new learning into the classroom or office:

One flaw in many PD or training sessions is the lack of follow through and continuous engagement, reflection, and improvement in the area of focus. While participants in the PD may gain insight and ideas, the probability that they will use this information long-term and will actively seek to better their practice as it relates to this topic are quite low. It is therefore essential that leaders continuously and consistently circle back to the topic. This can be done in many ways.

- Developing Professional Learning Communities (PLCs) and various professional partnerships that focus on discussion, reflection, and continuous analysis of data related

to trauma-informed practice.

- Incorporating the topic of trauma and language used in the common purpose and vision statement during staff meetings or activities.
- Purposefully including snapshot moments and/or creating team meetings that focus on trauma-informed practice.
- Including the topic and ideas, reflective pieces, and food for thought during conversational "coffee talk" moments with staff members.
- Creating a culture of professional learners who are inquisitive, motivated to learn more, and willing to share cases, new learning, articles and research, etc. by encouraging this in staff morale and engagement activities.

Home-School-Community relations:

Partnering with families, communities, and outside resources can prove invaluable when working with children and teens who have been impacted by trauma. Embracing and engaging these partnerships:

- Builds confidence and resilience
- Establishes trust
- Creates a sense of safety and care
- Improves school cultural
- Supports ownership and sense of agency
- Creates a connection and stronger sense of acceptance
- Provides families with the tools necessary to translate support from school to home

Engaging Family/Community	Engaging Community Resources
• Frequent positive communications home • Invitations to come support • Diversity fair • Themed nights • Child/teen-led and created plays or engaging activities • Parent/caretaker circles • Parent/caretaker training • Park/open space picnics • Read-aloud night/day (visit to local space that is easily accessible to families) • Restaurant nights • Community garden or volunteerism invitations • Sporting events • Game/carnival nights • Needs assessments and follow-up events	• Local library • Local YMCA • Local nonprofits • County government • Local business (restaurants, yoga/fitness/mindfulness studios, creative arts entities, small business owners as models or mentors, etc.) • Local free physical, mental, and financial assistance institutions • Local community college or higher education institution • Nature conservatories • Local minor league sports teams • Translators/interpreters • Local museums

When determining how to engage families and community, it may be beneficial to consider:

- logistics (time, space, ease of access for families who may have constraints involving: work, time, family commitments, lack of transportation, etc.),
- hindrances or hesitations that may lead to families unwilling to participate (cultural or language barriers, mistrust or unfamiliarity with staff, intimidation or discomfort, etc.),
- methods of communicating and marketing engagement opportunities,
- creativity in engagement opportunities,
- relaying specifics as to how families/community will benefit from engagement in these opportunities, and/or
- providing multiple modes of engagement (in-person, remotely, pre- or post-activity assistance, etc.).

Possible Topics/Outline of Talking Points for PD Sessions

The amount of time that can be dedicated to this PD, the level of intensity, and the opportunity for quality and consistent follow up, all are dependent on specific schools, districts, practices, and other professional organizations within the realm of your institution or practice. Due to the varying abilities and challenges that are unique to each community of professional learners, this section will simply provide a general outline of topics and talking points for trauma-focused PD. The time frame, level of intensity, and the specific structure of this PD will not be discussed, to allow for individualized determination based on needs and resources available to each organization.

The topics and talking points will be arranged in order of possible PD dosage. In other words, the list will start with possible introductory points of discussion, then will flow into possible topics to follow until conclusion, reflections, and follow-ups. This is a lengthy list and certainly can be modified, whittled down, or tweaked as needed.

Topics/Talking Points:

- Purpose, mission, and common understanding of "what, why, how" on a group and individualized level
- Ground rules and creation of a safe environment for learning and growth for the participants
- How to actively and critically reflect (individually and in groups)
- Recognition of individual culture, values, experiences, limitations, possible misinterpretations, and biases that may impact understandings, mindset, and relationships
- How to engage in a professional learning environment when dealing with challenging subjects
- What is trauma?
- Types of trauma
- Impact of trauma
  - Physical
  - Neurological (mental and academic)
  - Academic
  - Emotional

- ° Spiritual
- ° Social
- ° Overall wellness
- ° Long- and short-term
- Globally-focused data on trauma
  - ° Prevalence
  - ° Long- and short-term impact
  - ° Populations
  - ° Etc.
- Data specific to the population with whom you work
  - ° Prevalence within the population
  - ° Predominant types within the population
  - ° Prevalent types within subgroups
  - ° Etc.
- Child development, attachment theories, and impact of trauma on the five key areas of development (cognitive, physical, social, emotional, and moral)
- Why this matters in our profession
- Why this matters for us as individuals in this profession
- How to create a trauma-sensitive lens
- "Looks fors" in children and teens
- Cultural implications
- Relationship-building and establishing rapport
- Language, tone, body language, and best communication strategies when working with children and teens who may have experienced trauma

- How to create a safe and comfortable environment
- Working with each other to create individualized care plans/roles and responsibilities
- Avoiding re-traumatization
- Balance of control
- Best practices and evidence-based approaches
- Educating children and teens on topics such as the brain, resiliency, grit, and impact that these positive elements have on overall long- and short-term well-being
- Strategies for shifting negative thoughts and negative self-talk
- Encouragement, confidence, and resilience-building
- Calming techniques and coping skills
- Problem-solving and executive functioning skills
- Meaning making and creating positive individual narratives
- Safety plans and individualized plans or ideas that are specific to the population that you work with and to the resources available to you
- Community outreach and building alliances with caretakers, loved ones, family members
- Helper fatigue and self-care
- Community resources and access to outside supports
- What next?
  - ° How to use this information to strengthen your work

- ° Creation of measurable goals, action plans, and time frames
- ° Concrete and consistent plans for follow up (individual, team, whole group)

Possible Activities and Experiences to Include in PD:

- Icebreakers to increase connection and emotional safety within the group
- Deep-level questions for reflection and prompting points
- Ample process and reflection time (individual and group)
- Exit cards
- "Backburner board" for questions which require more information to answer, or those that are not relevant to the current topic

- Anonymous questions box to ensure safety and confidentiality when desired
- Movie/video clips and discussion points
- Breakout sessions and small groups
- Gallery walks and opportunities to share in a non-threatening manner
- Vignettes for reflection (individual and group)
- "What Would You Do?" scenarios and game show (in groups, so as to increase a sense of safety)
- Case study share outs
- Modeling and experiential activities
- Speakers/presenters from various community organizations

Compassion Fatigue and How to Avoid it

Those who work with children or teens who have been impacted by trauma may experience some level of compassion fatigue at times. Often confused with "burnout." compassion fatigue refers to a physical, emotional, or spiritual exhaustion that overtakes a person and the ability to experience joy or to feel and care for others (Figley, 1995; Ortlepp, K. & Friedman, M, 2002). The impact of compassion fatigue can be far-reaching and, interestingly enough, congruent with that of childhood trauma. According to Figley (1995), symptoms of compassion fatigue can manifest in a number of forms including:

- **PHYSICAL:** frequent illness, tiredness, weakness, lack of energy, dysregulated sleep, loss of or excessive appetite

- **PSYCHOLOGICAL:** Feelings of stagnation, despair, loss, of control, excessive self-concern

- **SOCIAL:** Lack of connection or desire to connect, rejection, separation, withdrawal, feelings of emptiness and loneliness

According to psychologist Shawn Goldberg, three skills that aid in combating compassion fatigue are awareness, balance, and connection.

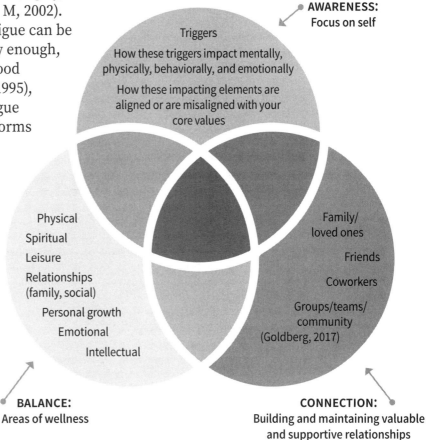

AWARENESS: Focus on self

Triggers
How these triggers impact mentally, physically, behaviorally, and emotionally
How these impacting elements are aligned or are misaligned with your core values

Physical
Spiritual
Leisure
Relationships (family, social)
Personal growth
Emotional
Intellectual

Family/ loved ones
Friends
Coworkers
Groups/teams/ community
(Goldberg, 2017)

BALANCE: Areas of wellness

CONNECTION: Building and maintaining valuable and supportive relationships

You may have already noticed some parallels between the impact of compassion fatigue and that of trauma. As such, many techniques that can be used to alleviate trauma could also be used to treat compassion fatigue.

The table below lists general techniques that may be used to combat compassion fatigue. Many of these techniques are reminiscent of those described in the "Snap Skills" section of this toolkit. Should you experience any level of compassion fatigue, it may be beneficial to reflect on these similarities, as well as on your own thoughts, feelings, and experiences, as this could increase your empathy, understanding, and connection to the children/teens whom you support.

Skills	Techniques to Combat Compassion Fatigue
Awareness	<ul><li>Identify triggers that lead to negative thoughts, feelings, or actions.</li><li>Recognize your physical, emotional, and behavioral response to triggers.</li><li>Understand personal vulnerability biases, and how they may impact your reaction to the pain or experiences of others.</li><li>Understand when to use specific "balancing" strategies based on the context and how each impact you.</li><li>Understand your locus of control, what is and what is outside of your control, and accept what you cannot control.</li><li>Recognize negative thoughts and challenge them with more helpful and healthy alternatives.</li><li>Be cognizant of irrational beliefs that may arise and counter them.</li><li>Make personal "stillness time" a daily essential.</li><li>Be cognizant of your telltale signs of overloaded, when to step back, and make a plan as to how you will step back.</li><li>Develop realistic expectations, for yourself and for others.</li><li>Remember that you are human and that you do not need to have all the answers or be everything for everyone.</li><li>Know your strengths, limitations, and align your work life with this knowledge.</li><li>Review how you spend your time and restructure your schedule as needed.</li><li>Create a "not-to-do" list.</li></ul>

Awareness *continued*	• Prioritize and filter out tasks that are stressful or unnecessary. • Be aware of and purposefully avoid negative forces (people, negative conversations/"water-cooler" talk, etc.). • Be aware of when you need to take a work break and plan how/when to do so each day. • Use "I messages," clearly state your needs, and be assertive. • Make the time to reflect on your successes, your progress, and things that you are grateful for.

Balance	• Apply deep-breathing strategies to calm your body and mind back to baseline. • Practice mindfulness and being in the present. • Use grounding techniques. • Understand your locus of control, what is and what is outside of your control, and accept what you cannot control. • Set boundaries, for yourself and others, delegate tasks, and ask for/ accept help" when you are overloaded. • Leave work where it belongs... at work. • Practice healthy sleep, eating, and hygiene. • Make regular visits to your doctors (GP, dental, skin, therapist, etc.). • Drink plenty of water. • Journal, create art, or find another creative release. • Set specific time for socializing, leisure, and personal-growth activities. • Move everyday – exercise, get outside, take time in nature, and soak in these moments with your senses. • Laugh daily. • Take time to get up and move, stretch, chat with coworkers, and get some fresh air at least 3 times during the workday. • Reconnect with your spirituality daily. • Practice daily gratitude. • Learn to "live simply" and avoid unnecessary, complex stressors. • Identify passions, hobbies, and set times to engage in these renewing and revitalizing activities.

Connection	• Seek advice and multiple perspectives.
	• Establish a strong support network at home, work, and other areas of your life.
	• Make the effort to establish and maintain diverse, positive relationships.
	• Join community teams, leagues, and events.
	• Take vacations.
	• Establish family routines and time for togetherness.
	• Communicate openly, honestly, do not pass judgement, and seek to understand varying frames of understanding.

Closing

—

Our children and adolescents are growing up in unprecedented times. Social, political, and civil unrest, a worldwide pandemic halting the safeties of daily life, a surge in the use of technology and access to social media, and numerous other modern occurrences have caused our youth to face a category of challenges that previous generations have never endured.

In addition to the perplexities involved with making sense of the modern world, our youth often face issues surrounding more individualized influences such as family, peers, community, and internal belief systems.

With a variety of spheres influencing wellness and development, the number of children and adolescents who have experienced mild to severe forms of trauma has risen exponentially. Now more than ever, it is imperative that we know how to support and guide our youth in cultivating resilience, grit, and overall positive well-being.

It is our hope that this book will prove to be one of the few that professionals will refer to time and time again.

PART 3
Appendix

Appendix

___

The Appendix includes sample activities from the accompanying Activity Guide for Children and the Workbook for Teens. Each set of activities is designed to help build one of the following capabilities: processing emotions, coping and grounding, resilience and boosting.

At the end of the Appendix is a detailed reference list as well as additional resources to find out more about the concepts addressed in this guide.

The instructions and access code can be used to download the handouts that accompany the sample activities provided on the following pages.

Instructions to Download Worksheets and Handouts

ACCESS:

https://www.boystownpress.org/book-downloads

ENTER:

Your first and last names

Email address

Code: 944882BRY785

Check yes to receive emails to ensure your email link is received

Activity Guide for Children and Workbook for Teens: Purpose and Use

T his guide is part of a set of resources designed to inform adults working with children and/or teens who have encountered trauma or hardships. The following pages provide additional detail and suggestions for using the supplemental resources as part of an overall trauma-informed kit to support youth.

Children and teens who have been impacted by trauma may benefit significantly from creative and diverse approaches to strengthening resilience and overall well-being. Art, movement, music, sensory, play, and various other experiential approaches that encourage reflection through creative platforms may provide greater opportunities for social, emotional, and cognitive enrichment. The benefits of supporting children and teens through the use of creative approaches are far-reaching.

Use of nonverbal, written expression, and various other creative approaches, provides an outlet for children and/or teens who:

- lack the cognitive ability to fully process and express orally or in writing,
- are developmentally unable to process and express orally or in writing,
- may have hesitations to express orally or in writing, or
- are unable to access implicit memory and the context of thoughts, feelings, or reactions that are stored in implicit memory.

(Hannigan, Grima-Farrell, & Wardman, 2019; Malchiodi, 2012)

Additionally, creative approaches allow children and/or teens the opportunity to:

- contain trauma or negative material within an object or artform that is safely outside of their own person,
- reduce emotional numbness or other dissociative coping mechanisms,
- feel a sense of connection and belonging by relating abstract or

metaphorical self-expression to a more universal theme,

- experience a more equitable platform for self-expression when the ability to hold a fair and balanced conversation with adults, caretakers, etc. is unfeasible,

- feel a sense of control over trau-matic or negative memories and emotions,

- set their own pace and avoid the anxieties of working under someone else's ideals,

- explore healthy and helpful relaxation strategies in order to reduce hyperarousal or chronic stress,

- feel a sense of empowerment, agency, and accomplishment,

- slowly gain exposure, which increases tolerance and ability to face experiences with confidence and grit,

- enhance problem-solving skills, and/or

- strengthen confidence, self-esteem, and emotional regulation.

(Baker, Metcalf, Varker, & O'Donnell, 2017; Malchiodi, 2012)

The accompanying *Workbook for Teens* and *Activity Guide for Children* serve to reach children and teens at their develop-mental, emotional, and cognitive levels using creative and reflective approaches. Each activity aligns with techniques out-lined in the "Snap Skills" section of this guide, and each is purposeful in targeting the areas of: (a) processing feelings,

emotions, behaviors, and actions, (b) coping, grounding, and calming, and (c) confidence-boosting, strength, and resilience. The expressive and creative activities included in these workbooks cater to a broad range of individual learning styles, skills, and needs.

Considerations/Food for Thought:

- Allow the child/teen to set the pace and tone.

- Do not force the child/teen to complete the activities, to create in a way that meets your expectations, or discuss their creation upon completion.

- Allow the child/teen to take control, and do not give unnecessary directions (although a few directives may be appropriate).

- Do not provide praise during the activity; rather, wait until they have told you that they are finished.

- Do not ask leading or probing questions.

- Allow quiet reflective time to occur, let the child/teen lead conversations, and ask open-ended questions.

- Do not make assumptions or pass judgment.

- Remind the children/teens that there is no "right or wrong," that these activities are whatever they choose to make them, and that they may take them wherever they would like to take them.

(Malchiodi, 2012; Wait & Ryan, 2019)

The activities on pages 71-80 are pulled from the Activity Guide for Children. *These are adult-led activities.*

Worry Worms

Purpose:

- Identify and process worries.
- Explore coping strategies.

What you will need:

- *Worry Worms* strips, or colorful construction paper cut into strips
- Markers, google eyes, and decorative materials
- Multiple copies of the *Worry Worms Photo Album* pages

Adult Instructions:

1. Reflect on the previous activities.

2. Provide the child with 5-10 construction paper strips, or allow him or her to cut out the *Worry Worms* strips provided.

3. Model how to fanfold these lengthwise so the strips resemble an inchworm.

4. Allow the child to add eyes and decoration to his or her worms.

5. Explain to the child that these are worry worms. Worry worms are squiggly and squirmy, much like the way our body feels when we are worried.

6. Ask the child what sort of things he or she worries about. Take turns sharing your worries.

7. For each worry, pull out one of the worry worms. If you'd like, you can provide names, characteristics, and funny stories about the worry worms. This helps the child to externalize, normalize, and add some creative humor and fun to his or her worries, which may make them less debilitating.

8. Use the worry worms and the descriptions of worries for each to spark conversation about coping mechanisms and strategies to ease worries for each worm. If you'd like, you may pull from the strategies provided in this guide or allow the child

to brainstorm his or her own personal strategies. If you'd like, you can write the worry and/or strategy to calm the worry on the worm itself.

9. You may choose to use the *Worry Worm Photo Album* below as a reflective piece to provide the child at the end of this activity. For each worry worm, copy a photo album page and use it as a discussion point. Staple and possibly allow the child to illustrate a cover page for the album if you'd like.

*NOTE   *Alternate option*

If you'd like, you could also have the child paint a plastic bowl to look like a halved apple (red on outside, seeds on the inside) to house his or her worry worm.

Worry Worms

Directions: Cut along solid lines, then fold along the dotted lines, fan-style.

Worry Worms Photo Album

Directions: Fill out below.

1. Name: __Wilber Wonderworm McWorm-a-worry__

2. Worry worm worry: _____
   Being home alone at night because mom works late.
   _____
   _____

3. Worry worm worry traits: _____
   Wilber Wonderworm McWorm-a-worry is scared and lonely.
   He cries a lot and thinks about his mom all the time.
   His body feels tense and shivery and his heart is sad.

4. How to calm this worry worm: _____
   Make a plan with his mom about safe and loving people he
   can call or have come over when mom is gone. Practice
   breathing strategies and think of happy things. Do something
   he likes to keep his mind happy (draw, game, movie).

Apple Dumpling

Purpose:

- Practice grounding, self-soothing, and reflecting on people, places, and/or things that youth can refer back to in times they need to calm.

What you will need:

- A warm and comfortable blanket
- One *Apple Dumpling* worksheet
  NOTE: You may also choose to create the same activity using play dough, soft felt paper, or any other craft medium
- (Optional) Ingredients for apple dumpling recipe (below), if you'd prefer
- One copy of the *Guided Visualization* handout

Adult Instructions:

1. Ask the children if they have ever seen/tasted an apple dumpling.

2. If the children have seen/tasted an apple dumpling, ask them to describe what it looks like. If they have not, explain what an apple dumpling is. Try to show them pictures, if possible.

3. Remind the children that an apple dumpling is a spiced and sweetened apple wrapped up in a blanket of sweet dough, then baked to create a warm and delicious treat.

4. Complete the *Apple Dumpling* worksheet with the children.

5. Lead the children through the *Guided Visualization* handout. To start, place the blanket on the floor. As you read the paragraph starting with: "Feel the gentle hands that softly lift you up and lay you in the middle of this comfortable airy blanket of dough," be sure to allow the children the opportunity to roll onto the blanket and envelope snuggly inside, as if they are the apple being blanketed by the dumpling dough.

6. Once you have completed the guided visualization, use the questions as prompts to discuss how mini-mind vacations can be used at any time to calm and ground themselves when they are feeling elevated.

Apple Dumpling

Directions:

1. Allow the children to color and cut out both the apple and the dumpling sheet.

2. Next, ask them to place the apple in the middle of the dumpling sheet.

3. On each corner of the dumpling sheet, they may write or draw one mini-mind vacation that they can take when they need a moment away. This can be something silly, like making themselves into an apple dumpling or pretending that they are a unicorn riding on cotton-candy clouds, or they can make it a place that they feel the most comfortable and warm, like the swing set at their favorite park or at their favorite restaurant.

4. Fold each corner of the dumpling sheet up so that it blankets the apple.

5. Explain to the children that they can carry this with them as a reminder of the things that make them feel warm, loved, safe, and happy. Tell them to think of these things whenever they feel anything undesirable.

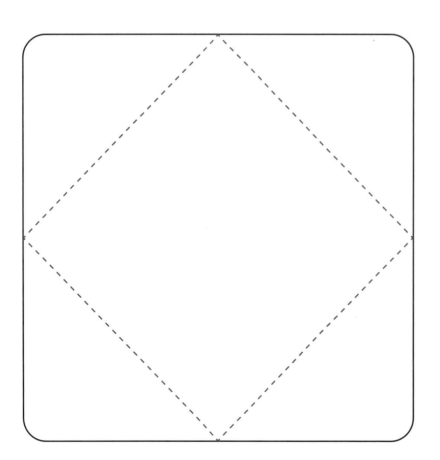

Guided Visualization

Get into a position that is comfortable for you. Maybe you want to lay on your back or stomach. Maybe you want to sit and put your head down. You may notice that there is a blanket unfolded on the ground as well. We will be using this blanket later on.

Close your eyes and take a slow, deep breath. The kind of breath you take when you smell a fresh batch of ooey, gooey apple dumplings getting pulled from the oven.

Slowly in through your nose.

Slowly out through your mouth.

Keeping your eyes closed and your breaths slow and deep.

Let's take a mini vacation in our minds. We are going to pretend that you are somewhere else and something else. I am going to guide you through this mini vacation with my words. As I speak, I want you to keep your eyes closed and try to imagine my words as a movie in your mind. Try to picture the story as you hear it. Try to imagine this story as if you were living it.

Imagine that you are an apple. A sweet, crisp apple freshly picked from your tree. Feel the cool, crisp orchard air on your skin. Imagine how fun the ride would be as you get plucked from your tree, placed in a basket, and walked to the front porch of a farmhouse. Try to imagine what you would see along the way. Would you see mountains? Fields? Farm animals? What would you hear? Would you feel the wind whistling by? Would you hear the farmer whistling a happy tune? Would you hear the farm animals chattering and galloping?

Let's keep breathing.

Slowly in through your nose.

Slowly out through your mouth.

Now, imagine that you have been gently placed onto the kitchen table. Can you feel the smooth and cool table beneath you?

You watch as flour, sugar, milk, and eggs get mixed, kneaded, and rolled into a soft and pillowy blanket for you.

Feel the gentle hands that softly lift you up and lay you in the middle of this comfortable, airy blanket of dough.

NOTE *At this point, you may stop and ask the children if they would like to roll into the blanket and wrap themselves into it.*

Smell the warmth of cinnamon and sugar as it sprinkles over you like sweet and spicy snowflakes. Feel the softness of the dumpling blanketing over you, protecting you.

Discussion/Follow Up:

Once the children have opened their eyes and are ready to talk, ask them:

- Does your body feel differently now than when we first started the story?

- What does your body feel like now?

- How did the deep breaths make you feel?

- How did sitting comfortably with your eyes closed make you feel?

- How do you think breathing and sitting like this could help you in times that you feel sad, angry, or upset?

Next, move on to the story.

- How did you feel as you imagined?

- How did you feel once you were wrapped in your warm, dumpling-dough blanket?

- What made you feel this way?

- Pretend that you have a cozy cocoon of your own. You can close your eyes if it helps you to create a picture in your mind. Describe your cozy cocoon to me.

- What do you see inside of your cozy cocoon (colors, items, people, etc.)?

- What do you hear inside of your cozy cocoon (music, nature, etc.)?

- What do you feel inside of your cozy cocoon (soft, fuzzy, warmth, etc.)?

- What do you smell inside of your cozy cocoon (vanilla, cake, etc.)?

Apple POP!

Purpose:

- Identify negative thoughts, experiences, or sources of unwelcomed feelings.
- Release unwelcome feelings, thoughts, and emotions.

What you will need:

- Red, green, and yellow (apple colored) balloons
- Markers that can write on balloons

Adult Instructions:

1. Reflect on previous activities.

2. Discuss how we sometimes carry negative thoughts, feelings, and emotions with us that may be caused by one, or many, experiences. Discuss why this is not a good thing to carry.

3. Explain that, today, you will identify some of the negative experiences and unwelcome thoughts, feelings, or emotions that you may carry. Share that you will reflect on how big or small these things are, or how much they fill up our mind space, and will find a way to release them in order to allow for more positive thoughts to fill our mind space.

4. Hand the children 3-5 balloons. They may have more if needed.

5. Ask the children to reflect on an unwelcomed experience or thought that has been filling their mind space. Tell them they have the choice to either share with you, or they may keep these reflections to themselves. If needed, provide examples of negative thoughts, feelings, emotions, or experiences.

6. Once the children have an idea in their heads, ask them to think about how much space this thing takes up in their mind. Does it take over their thoughts often? Is it just there sometimes but not too big? Is it the size of an apple seed or the size of a giant apple in their mind?

7. Ask the children to blow up one of the balloons to the size that they feel this is in their mind space (blow up just a little bit if it doesn't take up too much mind space, and so forth).

8. Tie the balloon for them as needed.

9. If they would like, they may use the marker to write or draw symbols to represent the unwelcome thought or experience on the corresponding balloon.

10. Continue doing this with the remaining balloons, or until they feel satisfied that they have identified all of their negative and unwelcome thoughts and experiences.

11. Reflect on the balloon sizes and the mind space they take up. Explain how these thoughts can quickly be blown into something greater and bigger than you'd like them to be.

12. Explain it is important to find ways to release these negative thoughts and to free up our mind space in order to allow in more positive, happy, productive, and overall better thoughts.

13. Using the previous activities as a starting point, brainstorm with the children ways they can release these negative thoughts in order to allow more positive ones to enter in.

14. Ask the children to pick up one of the balloons and identify at least one way they can release this negative thought. Once they have one in mind, allow them to squeeze or prick the balloon in order to pop it.

15. Continue doing so until each balloon is popped.

16. Reflect on the space these balloons take up now versus when they were full. Discuss thoughts that now have room to move in. Consider prompting with positive themes such as:
    a. ideas for self-care,
    b. goal setting and future-forward thoughts,
    c. points of gratitude,
    d. loving memories and image,
    e. jokes and laughable moments, and
    f. confidence boosters.

iRobot

The human mind and body are amazing things. We are almost like robots! Think about it...

A robot is controlled by an external force. Like a remote control or something that provides information and gives it commands. That robot then computes what is being asked of it and reacts accordingly.

If you want to turn your phone on for example, you press the "Power" button. What happens? It turns on! Maybe you want to search for the best local coffee shop. You pop into your Yelp app or just input the information you're looking for in your web browser and before you know it, the best latte spots are right at your fingertips!

Our minds and bodies kind of act in the same manner. We gather information from an external control (our environment, experiences, what is happening around us) and we use that information to activate our emotions and bodies to respond.

Just like our devices can glitch sometimes (miscompute data, get infected, etc.), our minds can glitch, too. We may misperceive data in our environment. That can impact how we feel, which then impacts how we react and respond.

Have you ever said "Hi" to a friend in the hallway, only to have them blow you off? Feels horrible, doesn't it? It makes your stomach drop. It makes your body go limp. It makes you wonder what you did to upset them. You respond by texting an angry and hurt "What did I do?" Then, you find out your friend had their earbuds in and didn't hear or see you. That is a mind glitch! You misperceived the data provided to you and it impacted your feelings and responses.

This happens more often when a personal trigger occurs. It may be someone raising their hand for a "high five," a loud noise, a facial expression, a word...there are a number of triggers that can send our minds back to a negative event that we experienced in the past, even if the present experience is nothing like what we had experienced before. These triggers impact our feelings and our responses in ways that may be disconnected to the present and in ways that are hurtful or unhealthy.

This is why it is important we recognize our triggers and how they impact our feelings and responses. If we recognize what triggers us, we can avoid that initial negative thought, which would then avoid a hurtful or unhealthy response. Mind glitch, averted!

Purpose:

- Recognize triggers, and their physiological and their emotional impact
- Identify the thoughts that accompany triggers

Directions:

1. Use the chart below to identify your triggers. When they occur, jot them down.

2. Pay careful attention to your body in these moments. Write down what you are physically feeling in the moment that you are triggered. Sometimes, it helps to close your eyes and pretend like there is a spotlight on each part of your body. Place the spotlight on your head and focus on what you are feeling in that area only. Then, move the spotlight to your neck, shoulders, chest...

3. Be mindful of your inner self-talk in the moment. Write down quotes that your mind is telling you. In the next activity, we will learn how to challenge these thoughts, how to counter the triggers and thoughts, and how to respond in a positive and healthy way.

Example:

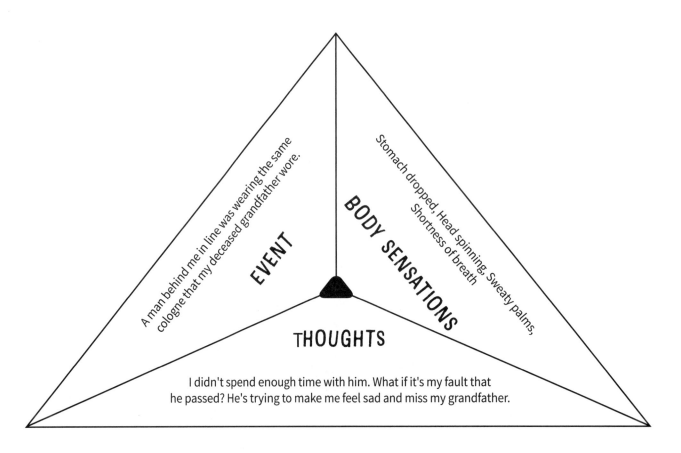

EVENT

A man behind me in line was wearing the same cologne that my deceased grandfather wore.

BODY SENSATIONS

Stomach dropped. Head spinning. Sweaty palms, Shortness of breath

THOUGHTS

I didn't spend enough time with him. What if it's my fault that he passed? He's trying to make me feel sad and miss my grandfather.

Swing, Sway, Oscillate, Pendulate

Have you ever seen one of those shows where a magician uses a pendulum (an object attached to a string that slowly sways back and forth) to make someone cluck like a chicken? It's always good for a laugh. The reason why they use a pendulum though, is because the movement, swaying slowly to and fro, can be a peaceful, tranquil, and mesmerizing movement. It can alter one's emotions and thoughts to drift and move from negative to positive and calm.

The calming technique we will explore today involves breathing, timing, and mind swaying back and forth until balance is found. We know that breathing is a powerful tool for calming our minds, bodies, and for preparing our brains to respond to unwelcome situations in a positive way. We are now going to expand on that by adding in the connection of breathing to timing, and by using that connection as we drift back and forth in our minds until we reach a strong mental balance.

Purpose:

- Practice a simple grounding technique
- Understand how to pendulate in order to achieve emotional balance

What You Will Need:

- One piece of string or yarn (about 12-15 inches in length)
- One hardware store nut, heavy bead, or something somewhat weighty that you can easily tie to the string

Directions:

1. To begin, create your pendulum by tying one end of the string to your chosen object. Be sure this object is weighty enough to produce a lasting and smooth swinging motion when you hold the opposite end of the string and gently move your fingers in slight sway motions.

2. Allow the pendulum to move in a gentle swaying motion.

3. As you track the movement of the pendulum, swaying under your control in your fingertips, focus on two things:

    a. The swing and sway of the pendulum
    b. The way your breathing sways with the pendulum

4. Breathe slowly in through your nose for 3 full swings, then out through your mouth for 4 full swings (in 1-2-3... out 1-2-3-4).

5. Allow your mind to drift in this moment. Drift away from any overwhelming or unwelcomed thoughts. Let the sway of the pendulum align with your breathing and move you toward positive thoughts and feelings. Drift toward happiness, positivity, and calm. Welcome and accept these feelings. Stay in this moment.

6. Now, allow your mind to drift in the opposite direction. Let the sway of the pendulum align with your breathing and move you towards the thoughts and feelings that can sometimes make you feel overwhelmed, upset, or uncomfortable. Welcome and accept these feelings. Stay in this moment.

7. Continue to sway back and forth in your mind, between these feelings. Focus on your breathing and how these feelings impact your emotions and your body, and welcome these feelings on both sides of the pendulum swing.

8. Once you are comfortable and accepting of both sides, find your balance, or the center point of your pendulum. Allow your mind to drift to a place where you are comfortable and confident in not feeling 100% well, nor 100% overwhelmed.

9. Reflect on how you feel in this balanced point. Consider the following:

    a. What does your body feel like?
    b. How is your mood?
    c. What emotions are you experiencing?
    d. What emotions did you feel as you swayed back and forth in your mind?
    e. When could this technique be helpful for you?

Kintsugi Bowl

Kintsugi bowls are artistic representations of the imperfections, broken pieces, and bad experiences that can be turned around to become things of beauty instead of things of shame or anger. Originating in Japan, these bowls are literally broken shards of a bowl, glued together with beautiful gold repairing glue, and transformed into a stunning work of art.

Purpose:

- Reflect on experiences and the positivity derived from them
- Strengthen self-esteem and ability to recognize strengths

What You Will Need:

- One clay, ceramic, or paper bowl
- If using clay or ceramic bowl:
    - One plastic baggie big enough to hold the bowl
    - Hammer
    - Strong glue (preferably gold in color)
- Paint, glitter, and decorative materials
- If using paper bowl:
    - Scissors
    - Strong glue (preferably gold in color)
    - Paint, glitter, and decorative materials

Directions for Clay or Ceramic Bowl:

1. Place the bowl inside of the plastic baggie and zip shut.

2. Carefully tap the bowl with the hammer, making large breaks in the bowl. Try not to create too many breaks or too small of breaks as this will make putting the bowl back together very difficult.

3. Using the paint, glitter, and decorative materials, decorate each piece of the bowl. You can decorate them to be similar, different, representative or symbolic, whatever you would like.

4. Carefully glue the pieces back together, creating the bowl again. This may take some time, patience, and re-gluing.

5. If you cannot find gold glue, you may choose to sprinkle glitter onto the glue before it dries.

Directions for Paper Bowl:

1. Cut the bowl into pieces with your scissors. They can be various shapes, sizes, swirly, straight, or jagged cuts, anything you'd like. Make the pieces almost like puzzle pieces.

2. Using the paint, glitter, and decorative materials, decorate each piece of the bowl. You can decorate them to be similar, different, representative or symbolic, whatever you would like.

3. Carefully glue the pieces back together, creating the bowl again. This may take some time, patience, and re-gluing.

4. If you cannot find gold glue, you may choose to sprinkle glitter onto the glue before it dries.

Keep your finished work of art as a reminder. The flaws, bad experiences, or imperfections you may see within yourself only serve to make you a more unique and stunning person. Someone to be admired, respected, and looked at with awe and inspiration.

References for Follow Up and/or Professional Development Training

─────

American Psychological Association. (2020, February 1). *Building Your Resilience.* APA. https://www.apa.org/topics/resilience

Badenoch, B. (2008). *Being a Brain-Wise Therapist: A Practical Guide to Interpersonal Neurobiology (Norton Series on Interpersonal Neurobiology)* (Illustrated ed.). W. W. Norton & Company.

Baker, F. A., Metcalf, O., Varker, T., & O'Donnell, M. (2018). A systematic review of the efficacy of creative arts therapies in the treatment of adults with PTSD. *Psychological Trauma: Theory, Research, Practice, and Policy, 10*(6), 643–651. https://doi.org/10.1037/tra0000353

Brunzell, T., Stokes, H., & Waters, L. (2019). Shifting Teacher Practice in Trauma-Affected Classrooms: Practice Pedagogy Strategies Within a Trauma-Informed Positive Education Model. *School Mental Health, 11*(3), 600–614. https://doi.org/10.1007/s12310-018-09308-8

Changing Brains: Applying Brain Plasticity to Advance and Recover Human Ability. (2014). Elsevier.

Charney, D. S. (2004). Psychobiological Mechanisms of Resilience and Vulnerability: Implications for Successful Adaptation to Extreme Stress. *American Journal of Psychiatry, 161*(2), 195–216. https://doi.org/10.1176/appi.ajp.161.2.195

Citri, A., & Malenka, R. C. (2007). Synaptic Plasticity: Multiple Forms, Functions, and Mechanisms. *Neuropsychopharmacology, 33*(1), 18–41. https://doi.org/10.1038/sj.npp.1301559

Combs-Orme, T. (2012). Epigenetics and the Social Work Imperative. *Social Work,* 58(1), 23–30. https://doi.org/10.1093/sw/sws052

Cowan, C. S. M., Callaghan, B. L., Kan, J. M., & Richardson, R. (2015). The lasting impact of early-life adversity on individuals and their descendants: potential mechanisms and hope for intervention. *Genes, Brain and Behavior, 15*(1), 155–168. https://doi.org/10.1111/gbb.12263

Cutuli, J. J., Alderfer, M. A., & Marsac, M. L. (2019). Introduction to the special issue: Trauma-informed care for children and families. *Psychological Services, 16*(1), 1–6. https://doi.org/10.1037/ser0000330

Deering, D. (1996). Compassion Fatigue: Coping With Secondary Traumatic Stress Disorder In Those Who Treat the Traumatized. *Journal of Psychosocial Nursing and Mental Health Services, 34*(11), 52. https://doi.org/10.3928/0279-3695-19961101-26

Dweck, C. S. (2021). *MINDSET : NEW PSYCHOLOGY OF SUCCESS.* Ballantine Books.

Felitti, V. J., Anda, R. F., Nordenberg, D., Williamson, D. F., Spitz, A. M., Edwards, V., Koss, M. P., & Marks, J. S. (2019). REPRINT OF: Relationship of Childhood Abuse and Household Dysfunction to Many of the Leading Causes of Death in Adults: The Adverse Childhood Experiences (ACE) Study. *American Journal of Preventive Medicine, 56*(6), 774–786. https://doi.org/10.1016/j.amepre.2019.04.001

Gertel Kraybill, O. (2019, January 31). *What Is Trauma? What you need to know about trauma, and trauma therapy.* Psychology Today. https://www.psychologytoday.com/us/blog/expressive-trauma-integration/201901/what-is-trauma

Grabbe, L., & Miller-Karas, E. (2017). The Trauma Resiliency Model: A "Bottom-Up" Intervention for Trauma Psychotherapy. *Journal of the American Psychiatric Nurses Association, 24*(1), 76–84. https://doi.org/10.1177/1078390317745133

Hannigan, S., Grima-Farrell, C., & Wardman, N. (2019). Drawing on creative arts therapy approaches to enhance inclusive school cultures and student wellbeing. *Issues in Educational Research, 29,* 756.

Hanson, R. (2018). *Resilient: How to Grow an Unshakable Core of Calm, Strength, and Happiness.* Harmony.

Im, H., Rodriguez, C., & Grumbine, J. M. (2020). A multitier model of refugee mental health and psychosocial support in resettlement: Toward trauma-informed and culture-informed systems of care. *Psychological Services.* Published. https://doi.org/10.1037/ser0000412

Joseph, S. (2015). *Positive Psychology in Practice: Promoting Human Flourishing in Work, Health, Education, and Everyday Life* (2nd ed.). Wiley.

Yates, T. M., & Masten, A. S. (2012). Fostering the Future: Resilience Theory and the Practice of Positive Psychology.

Kuras, Y. I., Assaf, N., Thoma, M. V., Gianferante, D., Hanlin, L., Chen, X., Fiksdal, A., & Rohleder, N. (2017). Blunted Diurnal Cortisol Activity in Healthy Adults with Childhood Adversity. *Frontiers in Human Neuroscience, 11.* https://doi.org/10.3389/fnhum.2017.00574

Leitch, L. (2017). Action steps using ACEs and trauma-informed care: a resilience model. *Health & Justice, 5*(1). https://doi.org/10.1186/s40352-017-0050-5

Malchiodi, C. A. (2018). *The Handbook of Art Therapy and Digital Technology.* Jessica Kingsley Publishers.

Merzenich, M., Nahum, M., & Vleet, V. T. (2014). *Changing Brains: Applying Brain Plasticity to Advance and Recover Human Ability (Volume 207) (Progress in Brain Research, Volume 207)* (1st ed.). Elsevier.

National Center for Trauma Informed Care. (2011, June). *What's trauma-informed care?* SAHMSA. https://www.samhsa.fov/nctic/trauma.asp

National Council for Mental Wellbeing. (2020, December 18). *Integrated Health COE.* National Council. https://www.thenationalcouncil.org/integrated-health-coe/

National Research Council, Institute of Medicine, Children, B. Y. O., Development, C. O. I. T. S. O. E. C., Phillips, D. A., & Shonkoff, J. P. (2000). *From Neurons to Neighborhoods: The Science of Early Childhood Development* (1st ed.). National Academies Press.

Ortlepp, K., & Friedman, M. (2002). Prevalence and correlates of secondary traumatic stress in workplace lay trauma counselors. *Journal of Traumatic Stress, 15*(3), 213–222. https://doi. org/10.1023/a:1015203327767

Osofsky, J. D., & Lieberman, A. F. (2013). *Clinical Work with Traumatized Young Children* (Reprint ed.). The Guilford Press.

Rakes, C. R., Bush, S. B., Mohr-Schroeder, M. J., Ronau, R. N., & Saderholm, J. (2017). Making teacher PD effective using the PrimeD framework. *New England Mathematics Journal, 50*(1), 52–63.

Roozendaal, B., McEwen, B. S., & Chattarji, S. (2009). Stress, memory and the amygdala. *Nature Reviews Neuroscience, 10*(6), 423–433. https://doi.org/10.1038/nrn2651

Rose, R., Gray, D. D., Clerck, D. G. A. M., Wild, R., Crouch, K., Price, P., Tokunaga, S., Moore, J., O'Keefe, N., Mattiuzzo, A., Stokes, M., Marques, M., Barros, M., Otway, M., Park, J., Fasolo, A., LaSpina, S., Aulich, D., Saunders, E., . . . Morris-Jacobson, K. (2017). *Innovative Therapeutic Life Story Work: Developing Trauma-Informed Practice for Working with Children, Adolescents and Young Adults.* Jessica Kingsley Publishers.

Rothschild, B. (2000). *The Body Remembers: The Psychophysiology of Trauma and Trauma Treatment (Norton Professional Books (Hardcover))* (Illustrated ed.). W. W. Norton & Company.

Steele, W., & Malchiodi, C. A. (2011). *Trauma-Informed Practices With Children and Adolescents* (1st ed.). Routledge.

Substance Abuse and Mental Health Services Administration. (2014). *SAMHSA's Concept of Trauma and Guidance for a Trauma-Informed Approach.* SAMHSA. https://ncsacw.samhsa.gov/userfiles/ files/SAMHSA_Trauma.pdf

Tedeschi, R. G., Park, C. L., & Calhoun, L. G. (2014). *Posttraumatic Growth: Positive Changes in the Aftermath of Crisis (The Lea Series in Personality and Clinical Psychology)* (1st ed.). Routledge.

Trauma-Informed Care in Behavioral Health Services, a Treatment Improvement Protocol (TIP 57). (2021). U. S. Department of Health and Human Services.

The Truth About ACEs Infographic. (2018, June 20). RWJF. https://www.rwjf.org/en/library/infographics/ the-truth-about-aces.html

Ungar, M. (2014). Practitioner Review: Diagnosing childhood resilience - a systemic approach to the diagnosis of adaptation in adverse social and physical ecologies. *Journal of Child Psychology and Psychiatry, 56*(1), 4–17. https://doi.org/10.1111/jcpp.12306

Waite, R., & Ryan, R. A. (2019). *Adverse Childhood Experiences: What Students and Health Professionals Need to Know* (1st ed.). Routledge.

Useful Websites

https://www.pacesconnection.com/

Provides information, research, science, and resources regarding ACES and adverse experiences.

https://acestoohigh.com/

ACES too High provides news, research, and information on ACES and strategies to counter adverse experiences for individuals, families, professionals, and communities.

https://developingchild.harvard.edu/

The Center on the Developing Child at Harvard University aims to provide scientific and research-based evidence and education to improve the lives of children facing adversity.

https://www.samhsa.gov/child-trauma

SAMHSA's National Child Traumatic Stress Initiative (NCTSI) provides up-to-date evidence, research, and resources for parents, professionals, and community in order to support children and teens who have experienced trauma.

http://cctasi.northwestern.edu/

The Center for Child Trauma Assessment, Services, and Interventions at Northwestern University provides information and interventions to support children and teens who have been impacted by trauma.

http://www.traumainformedcareproject.org/index.php

This Iowa-based site was created to educate communities and caregivers on the impact of trauma, as well as on trauma-informed care.

https://www.nctsn.org/treatments-and-practices/core-curriculum-childhood-trauma

UCLA-Duke University National Center for Child Traumatic Stress (NCCTS) in partnership with the National Child Traumatic Stress Network (NCTSN), the Core Curriculum on Childhood Trauma, or CCCT, provides professionals with a detailed path towards trauma awareness, understandings, and skills to support youth.

https://www.blueknot.org.au

The Blue Knot Foundation, a part of the National Centre of Excellence for Complex Trauma, provides survivors, supporters, and professionals with a plethora of information and guidance in the areas of trauma.

http://traumatransformed.org/documents/tia_usf.pdf

This self-assessment can be used to inform next steps and areas of need when creating and sustaining a culture of trauma-informed care. The proper citation of this assessment would be:

> Hummer, V. & Dollard, N. (2010). Creating Trauma-Informed Care Environments: An Organizational Self-Assessment. (part of Creating Trauma-Informed Care Environments curriculum) Tampa FL: University of South Florida. The Department of Child & Family Studies within the College of Behavioral and Community Sciences.

https://www.ncbi.nlm.nih.gov/books/NBK207204/

This website would prove very helpful in the creation and sustaining of a trauma-informed community of professionals. It includes key areas to consider when creating, implementing, and following through with promoting a culture of trauma-informed care.